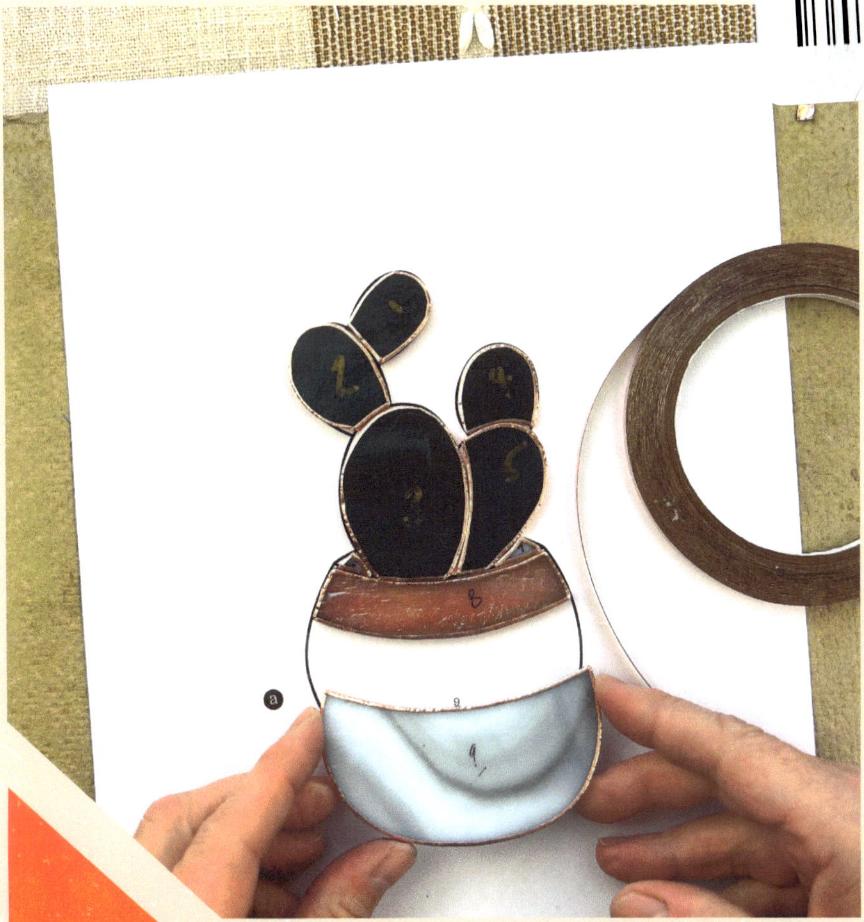

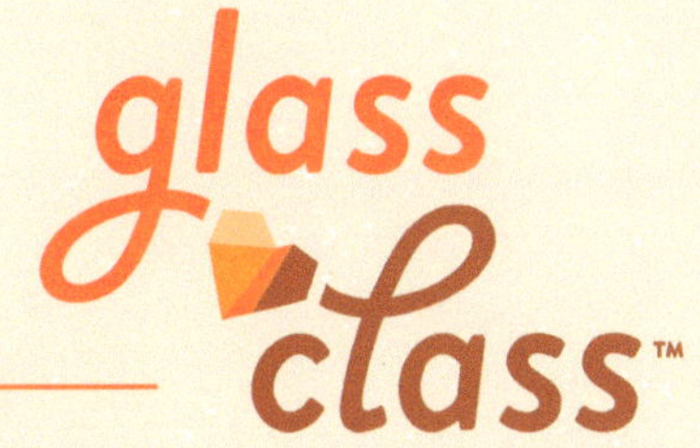

Stained Glass Suncatchers

24 Cutting-Edge Patterns and How to Make Them

AF255626

Copyright © 2022 Glass Class.
Heidi Wurm, Sarah Allgire, Hannah Jacobs

All rights reserved. This book or any portion thereof may not be reproduced
or used in any manner whatsoever without the express written permission of
the copyright owners except for the use of brief quotations in a book review.

The contents of this book are for personal use only. Patterns contained herein
may be reproduced in limited quantities for such use. Any commercial or
large-scale reproduction or production of works based in whole or in part
upon the designs contained in this book is prohibited without the written
consent of the copyright owners.

All other marks are the property of their respective owners.

Printed in the United States of America

First Printing, 2022

ISBN 978-0-578-28506-1

Glass Class
glassclasspatterns.com

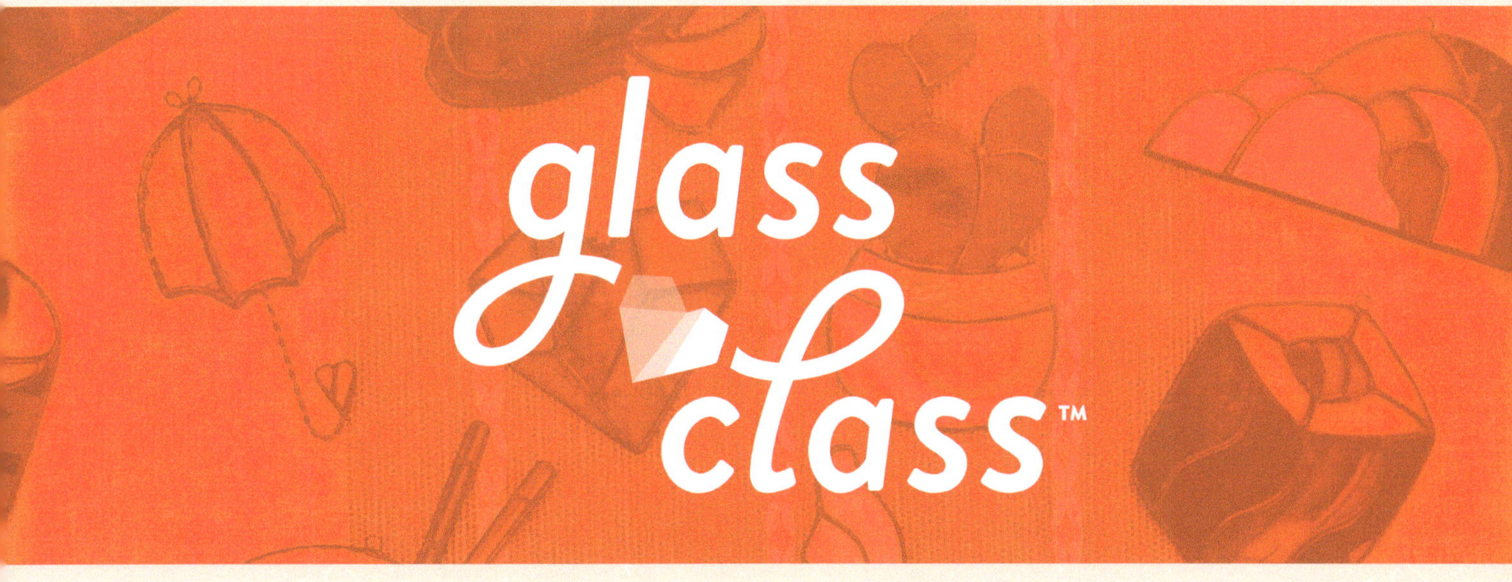

Stained Glass Suncatchers

24 CUTTING-EDGE PATTERNS AND HOW TO MAKE THEM

Glass by *Heidi Wurm*

Design by *Sarah Allgire* • Words by *Hannah Jacobs*

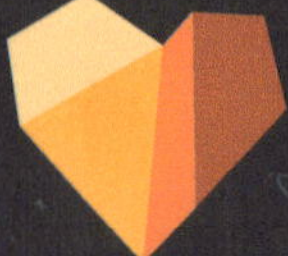

In memory of
Jill Ehrhart

Our beloved friend and honorary aunt:
Your laughter and love will live on in
the light that shines through each
piece created from this book.

Your memory is a treasure.

Who we are

Photo: Andi & Zoe Photography

Find this Koi pattern on page 60.

Heidi Wurm MAKER

Heidi is a studio-trained stained glass artisan with nearly three decades of experience in glass art and instruction, and is currently a resident artist at her local arts center. She's also an avid crocheter and has dedicated her time to teaching workshops, working in libraries, and supporting community nonprofits. Heidi also has more than 30 years of experience in motherhood as mom to her co-authors Sarah and Hannah and their brother Seth. She raised them to believe they could be anything — or create anything. Her life motto is: "We can make that." She finds great joy in a pot of strong, black coffee and in sharing her love of handcrafted art with her children, grandchildren, friends, and now you, our readers.

Sarah Allgire DESIGNER

Sarah is an experienced designer and creative professional. She created the design of each pattern in this book, as well as the design and format of the book itself. Sarah believes in the power of authenticity and design to make a positive impact, and she loves to dive into the details. She has spent years on the phone with her mother perfecting her stained glass patternmaking skills, adjusting angles and breaklines to improve both the form and function of a piece. Sarah loves language learning and exploring new places with her family — her travel dreams always include a long nap and a good book.

Hannah Jacobs WORDSMITH

Hannah is a communications professional and project manager with a decade of experience in corporate and nonprofit public relations, copywriting, and brand development. For this book, Hannah is serving as wordsmith (yes, currently writing in third person) and photographer. She runs our social media as well — follow us **@glassclasspatterns**! A mother of two, she enjoys reading, walking, Pilates, concert-going, amateur photography, and hanging out with her family and dogs.

◆ A NOTE FROM THE AUTHORS

We hope that you feel the love, empowerment, and positive energy we channeled into this book, and we can't wait to see what you create! **You can do this.**

Welcome to **Glass Class**

Whether you're an expert stained glass artisan or a new member of the stained glass community, you're in the right place. If you already have the tools and skills you need to fabricate, you can skip ahead to the ***Patterns*** section. If you're just getting started with stained glass — or if you need a refresher — we'll start from the beginning.

Table of contents

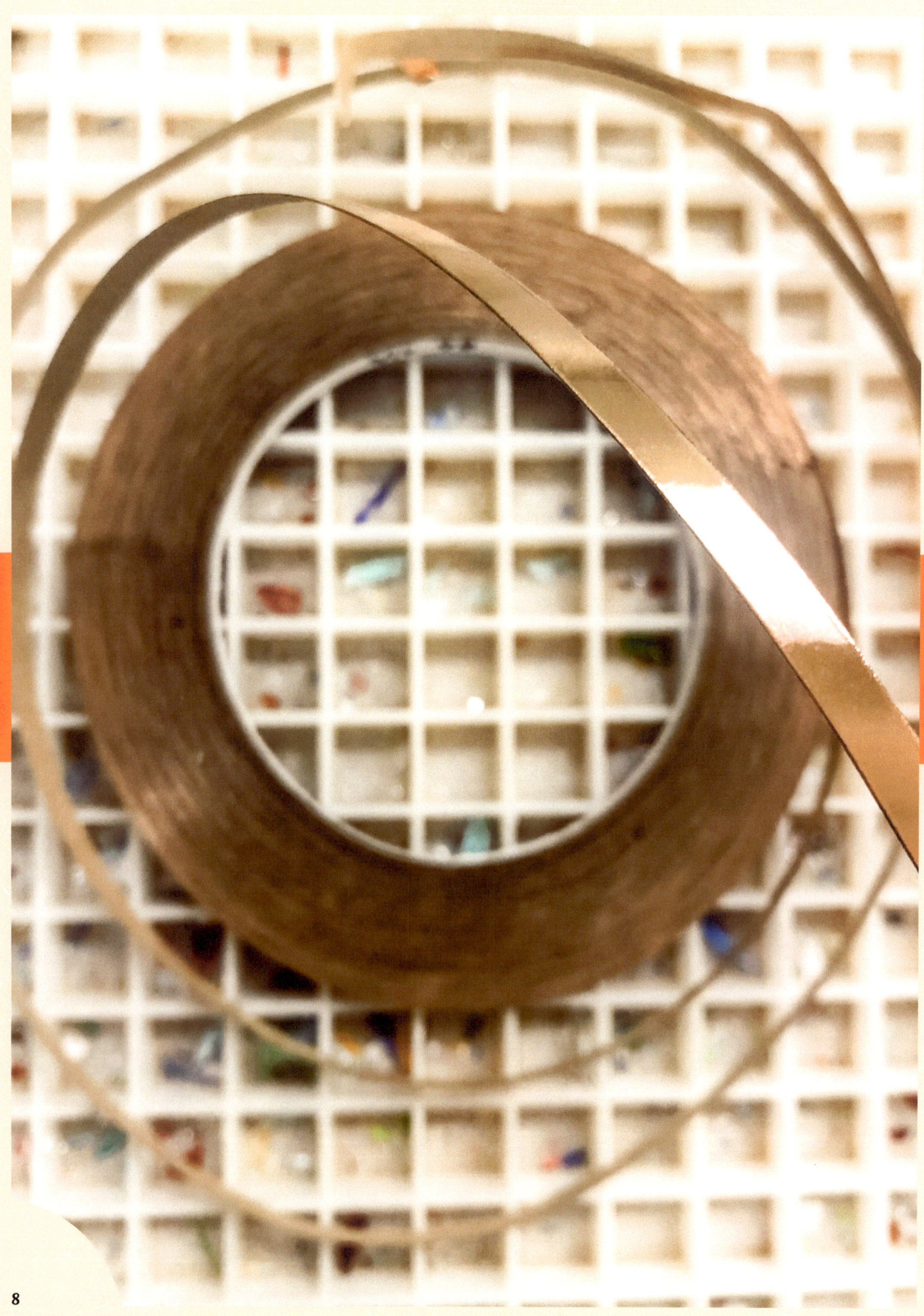

1 Suncatcher supplies

In this section, you'll find a carefully compiled list of everything you need to get started on your stained glass journey. This list is a reflection of Heidi's workshop and is based on her personal preferences for creating suncatchers using the copper foil method. If you prefer different materials or methods, stick with what you know.

While many materials are available online or at big box stores, we encourage you to support your local craft store or glass shop.

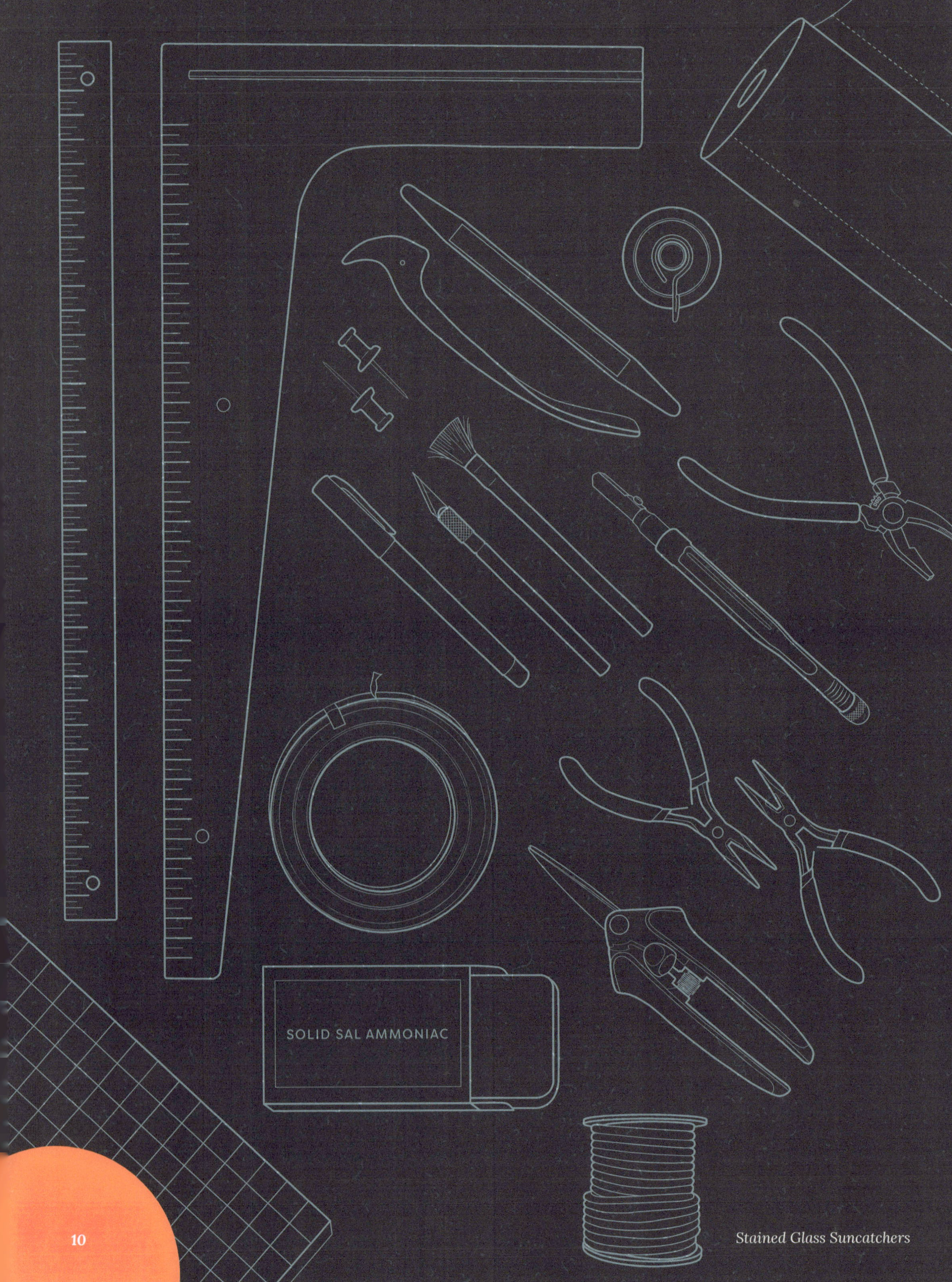

Stained Glass Suncatchers

Building your tool kit

If you're just getting started with stained glass, rest assured that these supplies are a valuable investment in yourself and your craft. If properly cared for, your tools will last for years to come.

PATTERN PREPARATION

- ☐ Stained glass
- ☐ Pattern
- ☐ Cardstock
- ☐ White copy paper
- ☐ Precision scissors
- ☐ Fine or ultra-fine point permanent markers or paint pens (black and metallic or white)

CUTTING & GRINDING

- ☐ Grinder
- ☐ Safety glasses
- ☐ Waffle grid cutting surface
- ☐ Glass cutter
- ☐ Glass cutting oil
- ☐ Straight cutting edge
- ☐ Grozier pliers
- ☐ Running pliers

⚠ *Use caution when handling glass and keep some bandages and first-aid supplies on hand. A few minor cuts and scratches are to be expected when working with this medium.*

FOILING

- ☐ 7/32" black-backed copper foil tape*
- ☐ Fid
- ☐ Precision craft knife
- ☐ Rubbing alcohol
- ☐ Paper towels

SOLDERING & WIRING

- ☐ 60/40 solid core solder†
- ☐ Soldering iron with temperature control
- ☐ Soldering iron stand
- ☐ Brass sponge with holder
- ☐ Sal ammoniac block
- ☐ Liquid stained glass flux
- ☐ Flux brush (acid brush)
- ☐ Heat-resistant soldering surface (cellulose-based fiber board or ceiling tile)
- ☐ Aluminum push pins
- ☐ 20-gauge pre-tinned copper wire
- ☐ 2 pairs of needle-nose pliers
- ☐ Wire cutters
- ☐ Metal O-ring

FINISHING

- ☐ Medium (grade 00) steel wool
- ☐ Patina (black for solder/lead)
- ☐ Stained glass finishing compound
- ☐ Soft-bristled brush (shoeshine brush)
- ☐ Gloves
- ☐ Rag for polishing

HANGING & CARE

- ☐ Fishing line or jack chain
- ☐ Eye hook or suction cup
- ☐ Non-ammonia formula glass cleaner or warm, soapy water

♡ Heidi's tip

Buy the best **glass cutter** and **soldering iron** within your budget. These are particularly worth the cost and will make a difference in the quality of your finished pieces.

Learn more about these tools on pages 14 and 15.

*** Optional:** 3/16" black-backed copper foil tape as described on page 15.

† Optional: 50/50 solid core solder as described on page 15.

All about patterns

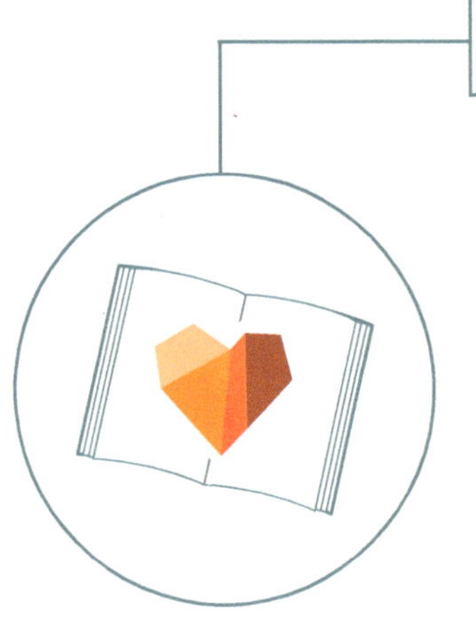

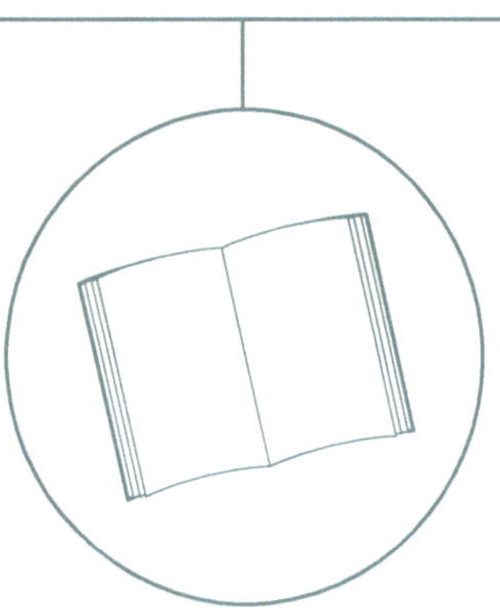

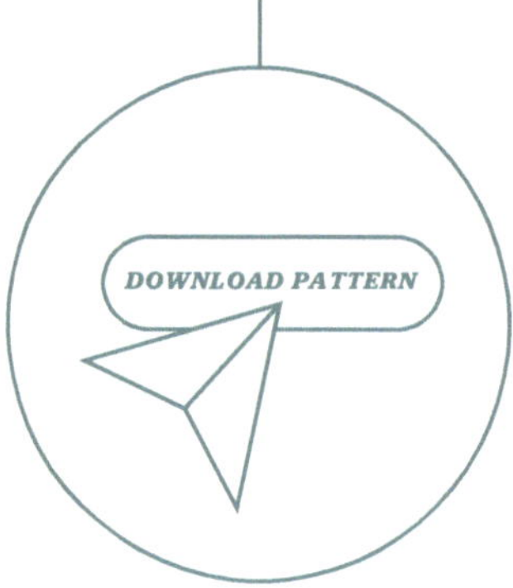

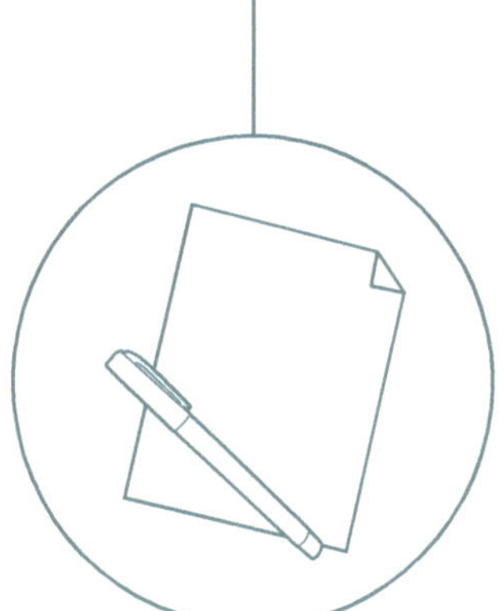

This book!

Visit **glassclasspatterns.com** to download bonus patterns.

Pattern books

Support your local library or craft store.

Online resources

You can find patterns available for free and for purchase online.

Make your own

Make sure your pieces can be easily cut. Pay particular attention to the breaklines of your pattern (the lines where the glass pieces meet). The way in which the pattern is broken up can change the entire mood or perspective of a project, but it's most important that it is physically possible (and preferably easy) to cut the pieces created by the breaklines.

WHAT TO LOOK FOR IN A PATTERN

Size and number of pieces

If you are a beginner, look for a pattern with fewer pieces and simple cuts to start. Consider the size of the final piece.

Curves and angles

Focus on the composition of breaklines and pieces — these elements add intricacy and detail.

Customization

Creativity can transform a pattern. Use an existing pattern as a starting point and modify pieces or add your own details.

Keep in mind that smaller pieces are also more difficult to cut. If too small, they can be obscured by the copper foil that overlaps the perimeter of each piece.

Consider the total number of pieces and overall size. The more pieces you have, the more complex and time-consuming your project will be. Large suncatchers can also be too heavy to hang with a suction cup.

How to prepare the pattern

If you select a pattern from this (or any other) book, start by making copies so you can cut out the individual pieces while preserving the original pattern page.

- Cardstock is best for the pattern copy. Thicker paper is more durable and will provide a structured template for tracing the pattern piece onto your glass.

- You can use plain copy paper for your layout guide, as it will be a reference for mapping and assembling your cut pieces.

Choosing your glass

CONSIDER THE FOLLOWING QUESTIONS:

?

Should the glass types be uniform or intentionally varied?

Texture and thickness of the glass can add detail and make areas stand out or blend in.

?

Do the colors of the glass complement the piece as a whole?

Color selection defines the character of the suncatcher. Consider tone, vibrancy, movement, and depth.

?

Do you have enough glass for the pattern?

Always allow space for breaking the glass and room for error.

Carefully consider cutability when choosing glass.

Thick or heavily textured glass can be difficult to cut and break, and it is particularly challenging with small pieces.

Smooth, evenly textured glass usually breaks more easily, which is helpful for patterns that require intricate cuts.

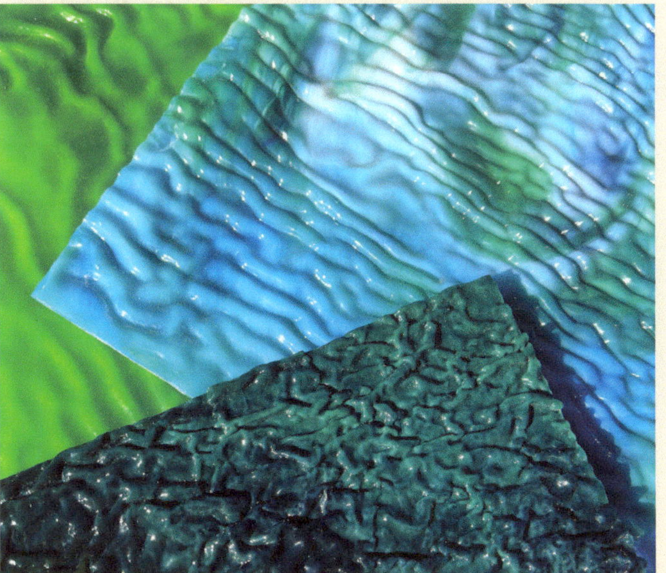

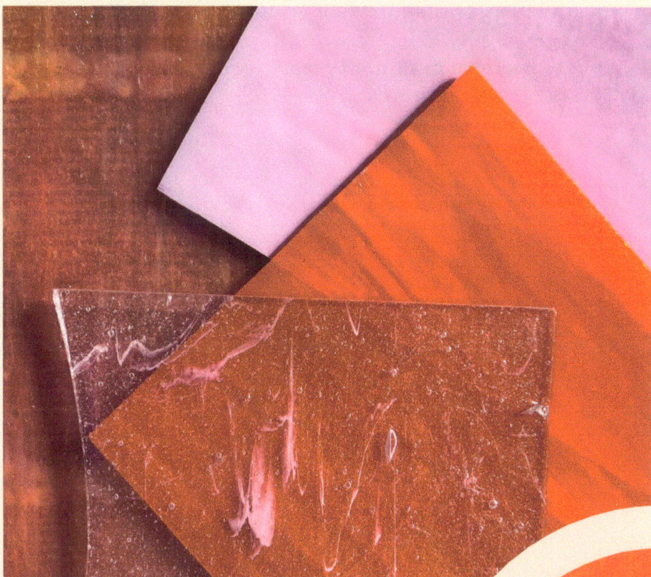

Choosing your tools

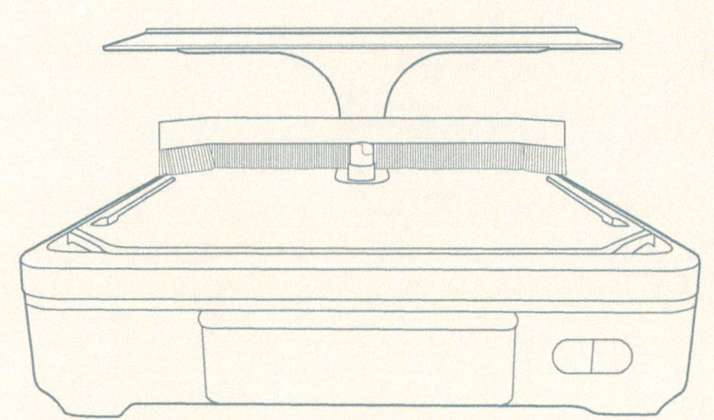

Finding the right grinder

A stained glass grinder is a power tool with a small, cylindrical diamond bit that spins rapidly to finely shape and smooth the edges of your glass (similar to sandpaper for wood). Most grinders used for stained glass have either a 3/4" or 1" grinding bit. Each size has its own value — a grinder with a 1" bit covers more surface area, allowing you to work faster. A grinder with a 3/4" bit works well for inner curves and details. Beyond standard sizes, smaller accessory bits can be used for even finer detail work.

- Set up your grinder according to the manufacturer's recommendations.

- Follow the manufacturer's instructions to maintain water in your grinder's reservoir. It acts as a coolant when grinding your glass.

- **Keep safety in mind!** Wear protective eyewear to avoid getting airborne glass particles in your eyes. Be careful with your hand placement as well.

Precision scissors

Choose a pair of small scissors with a sharp, pointed tip. This allows for a close, accurate cut when preparing your pattern pieces.

Glass cutter

A glass cutter is a handheld, pen-like tool with a small, sharp cutting wheel that creates a score line as it is pulled across the surface of the glass. The glass cutter needs cutting oil to lubricate the wheel as it moves. Lack of lubrication can lead to improper scores and chipped glass. Many cutters have a reservoir that is filled with oil. Turning the cap at the top of the cutter can open or stop the flow of oil. If choosing a cutter without a reservoir, be sure to dip the cutter in oil before each score.

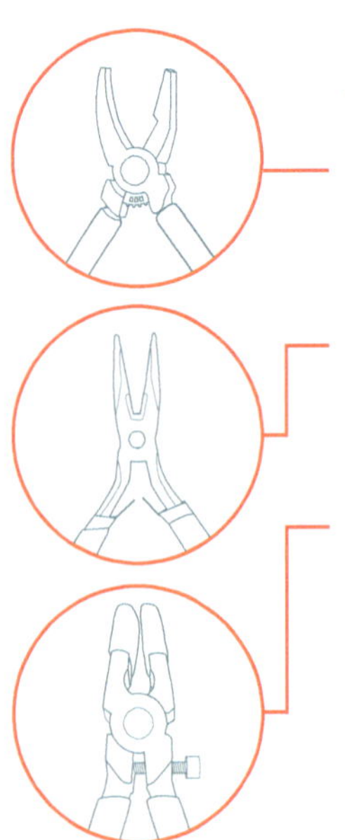

Pliers

Grozier pliers are specifically used to break glass in a controlled manner.

Needle-nose pliers are used to straighten wire and hold it in place while soldering.

Running pliers are used to break straight lines and are especially helpful when working with narrow pieces of glass. To use, line up the centering mark on the edge of the pliers and squeeze the handles gently but firmly. This should cause the break to run the length of your score.

Cellulose-based fiber board

This type of sturdy, heat-resistant board is an ideal work surface for any stained glass project. The density of the fiber board holds up to cuts, solder does not burn the surface, and chemicals (like flux) absorb safely. Find heat-resistant soldering surfaces at your local stained glass shop, online merchandisers, and even some home improvement stores.

Cutting surface

A waffle grid surface is ideal for cutting glass. When cutting, the glass shards will drop below your cutting surface, preventing the glass you're working on (and your hands!) from being scratched.

Fid

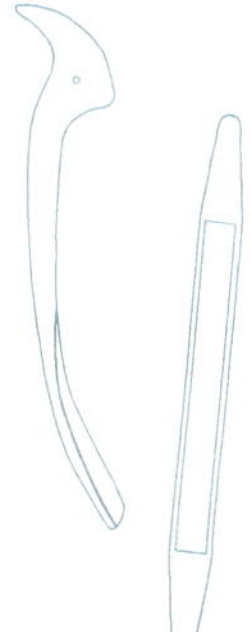

A fid is a uniquely shaped hand tool often made from wood or hard plastic. It can be used for many things in your stained glass workshop. As you make your suncatcher, you will use a fid to press down and smooth the adhesive-backed foil tightly to the surface of the glass. This process is called **burnishing**.

Foil

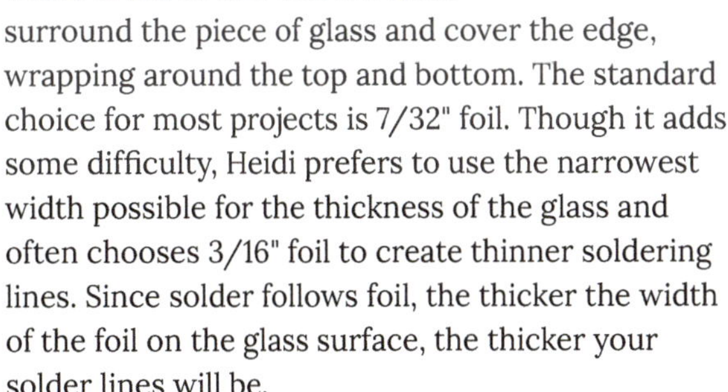

Copper foil tape is available in different widths. Glass thickness is a good way to determine which width of foil to use. The foil must surround the piece of glass and cover the edge, wrapping around the top and bottom. The standard choice for most projects is 7/32" foil. Though it adds some difficulty, Heidi prefers to use the narrowest width possible for the thickness of the glass and often chooses 3/16" foil to create thinner soldering lines. Since solder follows foil, the thicker the width of the foil on the glass surface, the thicker your solder lines will be.

We've recommended black to get started, but you can also find copper foil tape with different backing colors, like copper or silver. Use the backing that corresponds with the patina you plan to use. The color of the backing may be visible through the glass, so this small detail impacts your finished product.

Flux

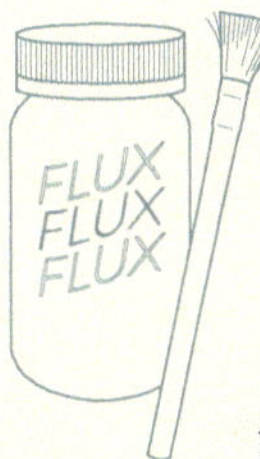

Flux is a chemical that cleans metal surfaces and allows solder to flow smoothly along its intended path. It's best to use a flux made specifically for stained glass. Flux should be applied frequently during the soldering process with a flux brush or acid brush. It's important to flux on a chemical-safe surface.

Soldering iron

It's best to use an iron designed for the stained glass industry. If your iron does not have a built-in heat control, you must have a separate unit (rheostat) to regulate the temperature. **Keep safety in mind when working with high temperatures!**

- Generally, your iron should be 80 to 100 watts with a metal element or 67 watts with a ceramic element.

- Look for a chisel tip (approximately 3/16"). This size allows you to cover the seams without extending into the unfoiled area.

- The iron should be well balanced. A tip end that is too heavy is difficult to keep level, which can cause hand fatigue.

Solder

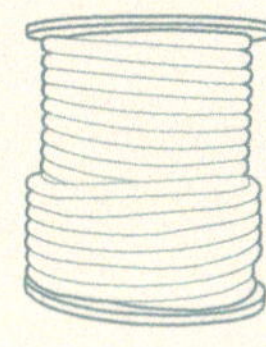

Solder is a low-melting alloy used to join together your foiled glass pieces. You'll use your iron to melt the solder and apply it along the seams of your pattern using three different techniques:

Tack soldering is the application of small amounts of melted solder on each joint to hold your pieces in place.

Flat soldering is an even application of melted solder along the copper foil that acts as a base layer.

Finish soldering is the application of the finish bead, which is a smooth, rounded layer of solder on the surface of each seam.

While not required, Heidi recommends using 50/50 solder to flat solder and 60/40 to lay your finish bead. The solder types melt at different temperatures, giving you more time to perfect the bead and work the area without melting the solder through to the other side.

Work how you want, where you want

A dedicated workspace is nice to have, but you can work on your stained glass project anywhere. Here are few things to keep in mind:

▶ **Stained glass can get messy.**

Tiny pieces of glass are likely to become airborne during the cutting and grinding processes, so remember to wear eye protection and use a grinder shield to help contain some of the debris. Small shards of glass often find their way to the floor of your workspace as well, so wear shoes while you work to protect your feet.

▶ **Work on a surface dedicated to your project.**

High temperatures and certain chemicals can be damaging to your space. Make sure to use the waffle grid cutting surface when cutting and breaking, and the cellulose-based fiber board when using chemicals or high temperatures.

▶ **Have a good light source nearby.**

Apart from being able to see what you're working on, stained glass itself can have a very different appearance depending on the lighting situation. Hold your glass up to natural or bright light to see how it shines through — this will more closely resemble your final product.

▶ **Find a space with proper ventilation.**

It's important to have good ventilation when working with chemicals. An ideal workspace should have open windows, high ceilings, exhaust fans, or smoke absorbers.

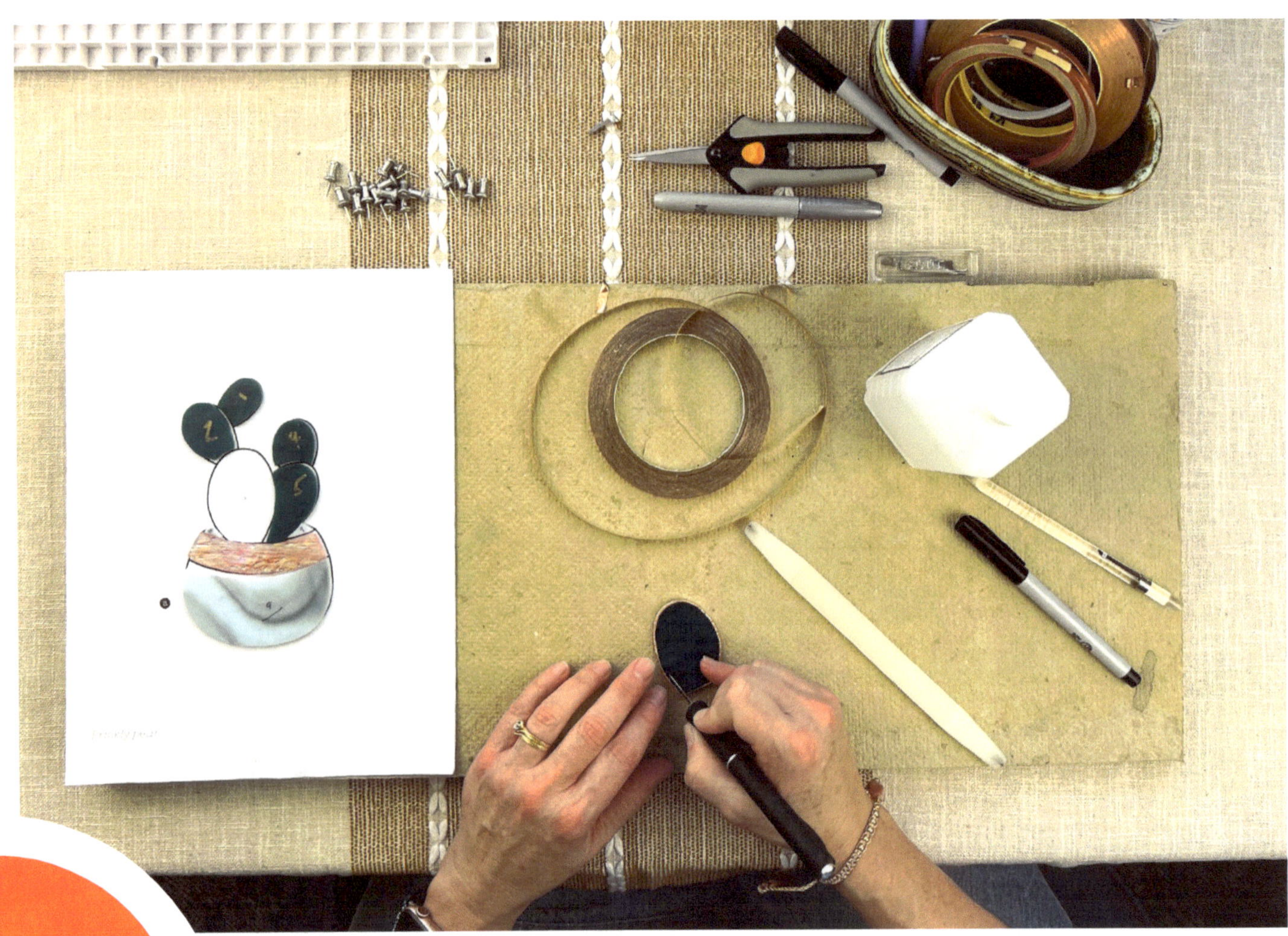

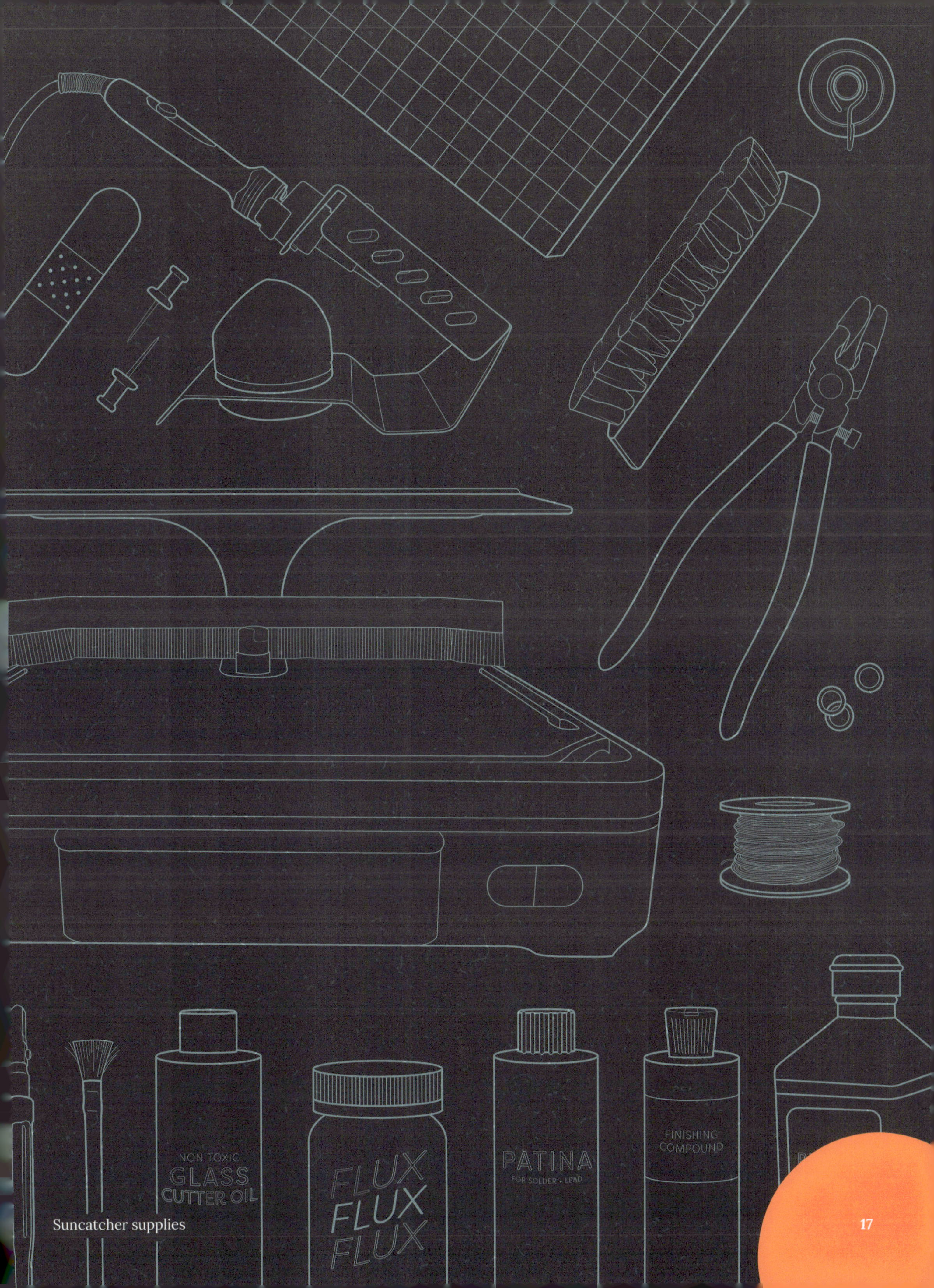

NON TOXIC
GLASS
CUTTER OIL
FLUX
FLUX
FLUX
PATINA
FOR SOLDER · LEAD
FINISHING
COMPOUND

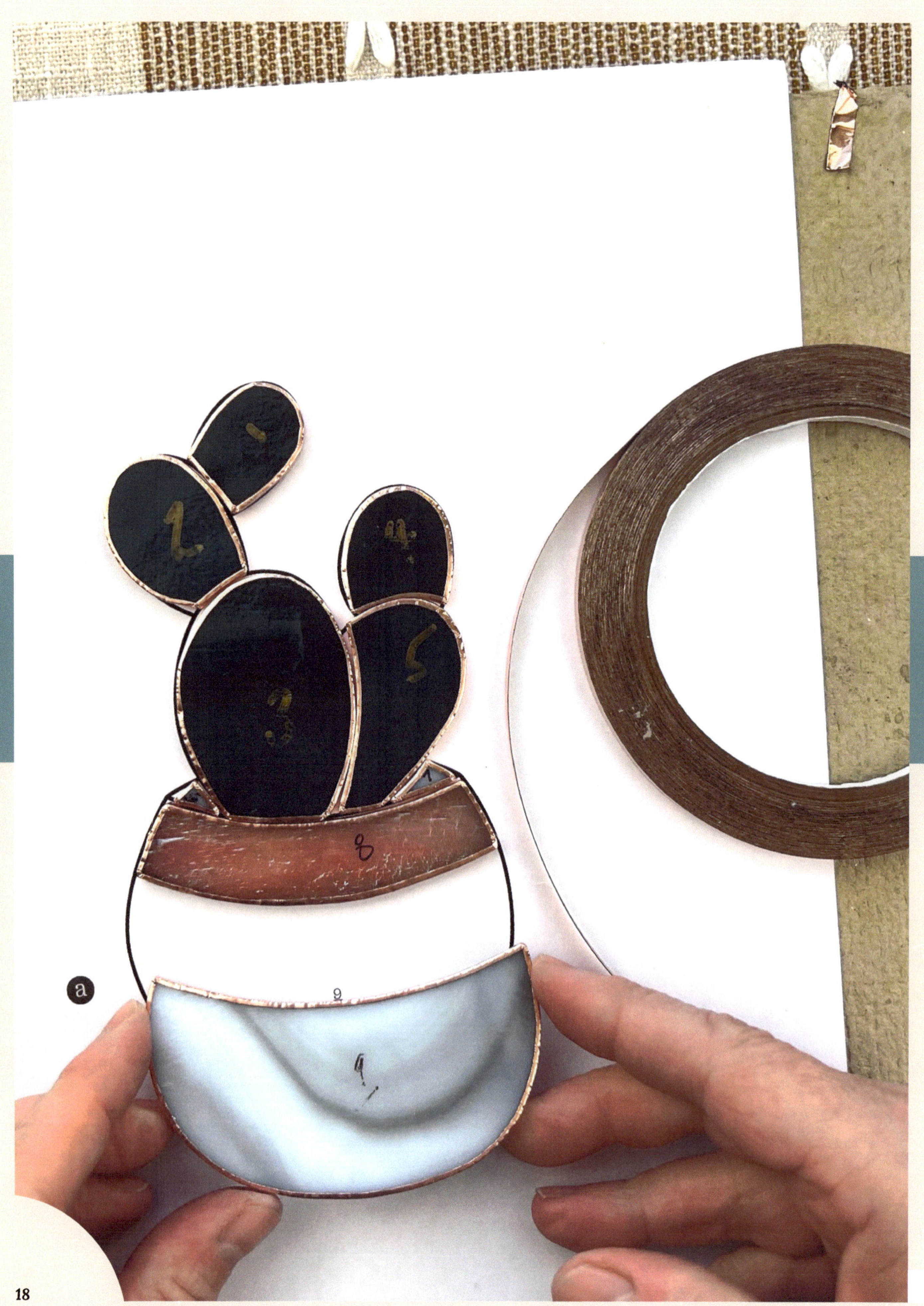

Preparation & process

GETTING STARTED

Now for the most important aspects of creating quality stained glass work: selecting your pattern, cutting the glass, grinding, foiling, soldering, and finishing. You won't want to skip this part — each step is crucial to the process.

If something isn't right early on, the issue can compound as you go. The quality of your pattern pieces affects the fit of the glass. Your scoring, breaking, and grinding will determine the quality of your foiling. Your foiling will determine where your solder flows. All of these elements are interconnected when creating your work of art.

◀ *Find this Prickly Pear pattern on page 51.*

Preparing your project

Supplies

▸ Stained glass ▸ Pattern ▸ Cardstock ▸ White copy paper
▸ Precision scissors ▸ Fine or ultra-fine point permanent markers/paint pens

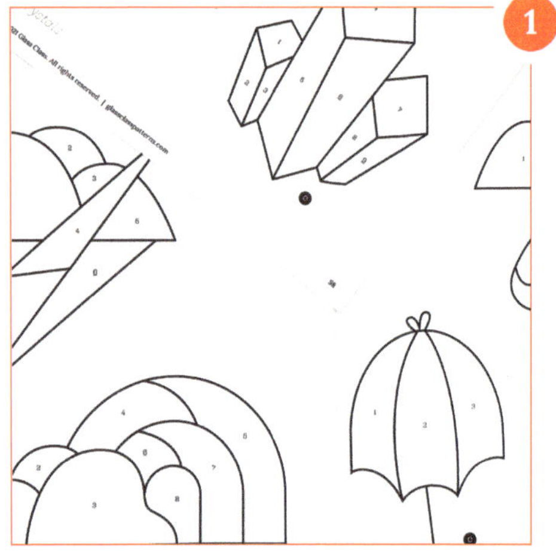

① *Pick your pattern*

Choose from one of the patterns in this book, find another, or create your own! These tips apply no matter the pattern.

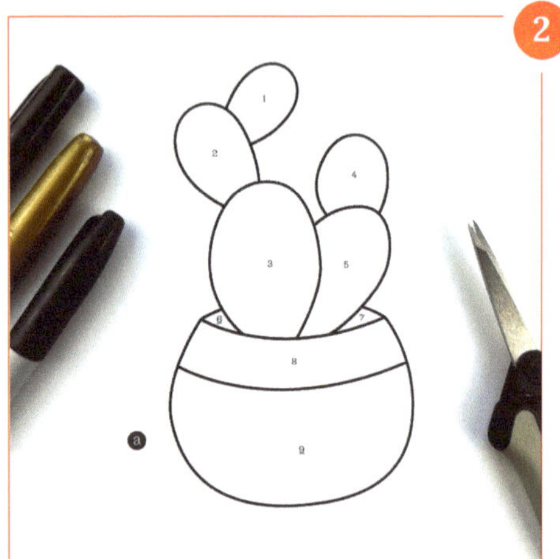

② *Number your pieces*

Each piece of your pattern should have its own number. If you select a pattern without numbers, you'll need to write them yourself. If you're using a pattern from this book, we've already added them, and you can skip this step.

(!) *Helpful hints*

THINK AHEAD

Number the pieces before making any copies so you only have to do it once.

SIMILAR NUMBERS

Underline your <u>6</u> and <u>9</u> so it's obvious which is which when your pieces get shuffled around.

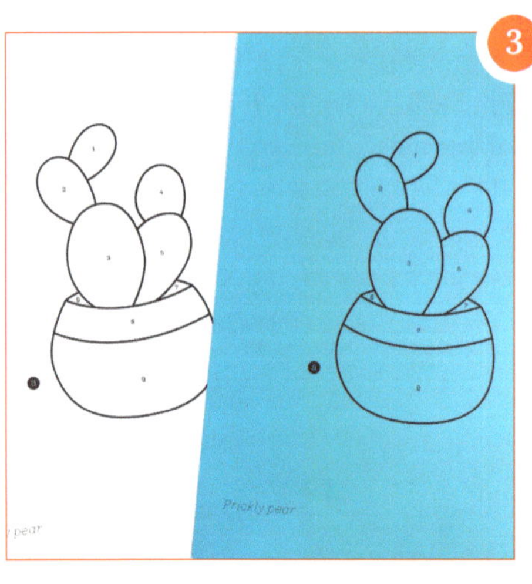

③ *Make copies*

In addition to your original pattern, remember to make two working copies:

▸ **Pattern copy**

Use cardstock to cut the pattern into individual pieces. These will be used to trace on your glass.

▸ **Layout copy**

Use regular copy paper — this will serve as your pattern guide when assembling your suncatcher.

You can reproduce the pattern by hand using cardstock and tracing paper, copy and print at home, or use a professional printing service.

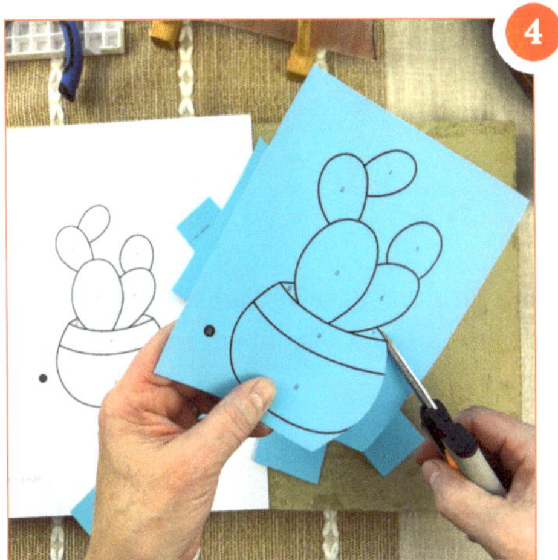

4 Cut out the pattern

Start with the cardstock pattern copy. Using precision scissors, completely cut away the black borders of each pattern piece.

The more accurate your pattern is, the more accurate your glass pieces will be.

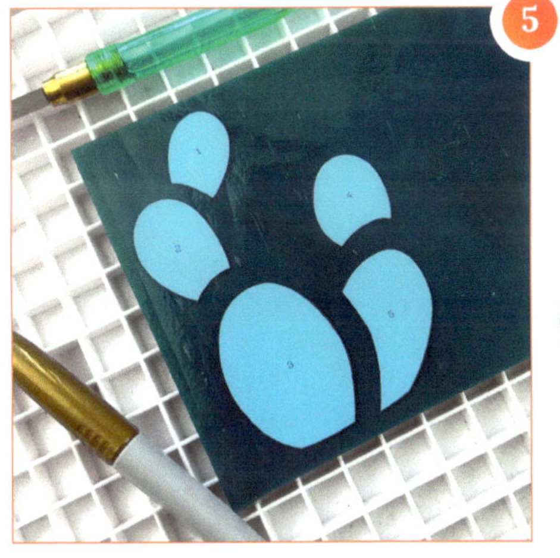

5 Lay out your pattern

Lay your pattern pieces face-up on the area of glass you intend to use. Color choice, transparency, and texture can all make pieces stand out or fade into the background depending on their placement. When laying out the pattern pieces, leave room to cut around and break the glass.

> **(!) Helpful hint**
>
> #### GO WITH THE GRAIN
>
> While it may not always be obvious, each piece of stained glass has its own grain and direction. Consider how the grain affects the movement of your finished suncatcher and position your pattern pieces accordingly.

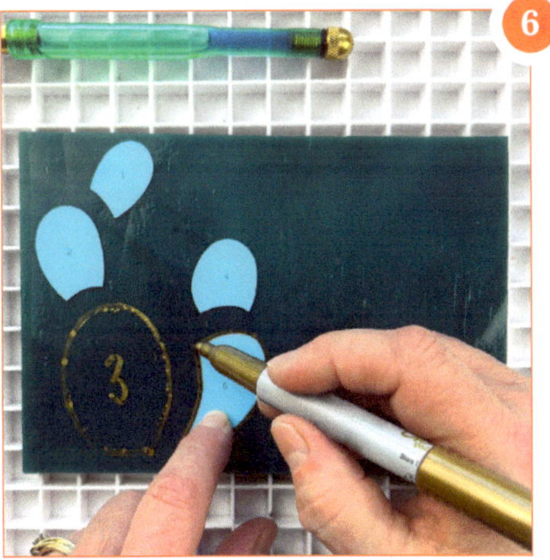

6 Trace your pattern

Use a permanent marker to trace the pattern directly onto the smoothest side of the glass, including the number. The marker will come off easily during the finishing stage.

Cutting and grinding

- ▸ Stained glass ▸ Grinder ▸ Safety glasses ▸ Waffle grid cutting surface
- ▸ Glass cutter ▸ Glass cutting oil ▸ Straight cutting edge
- ▸ Grozier pliers ▸ Running pliers

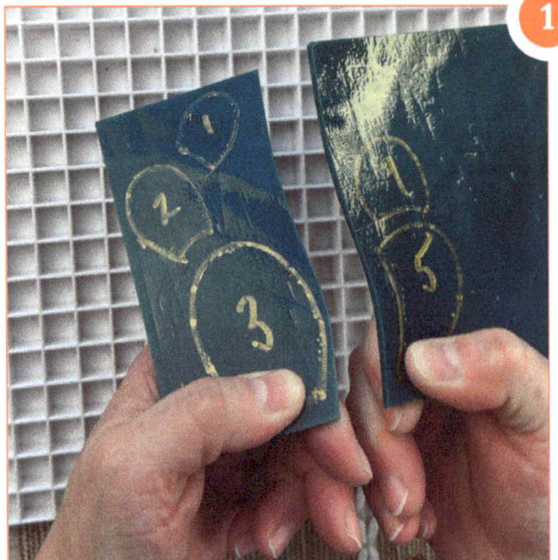

1 Create workable pieces for cutting

Once you have traced each pattern piece, split your glass into smaller, more manageable pieces. To do this, score and break the glass from edge to edge, leaving space for cutting around your pattern.

Review Steps 2 and 3 for proper scoring and breaking techniques.

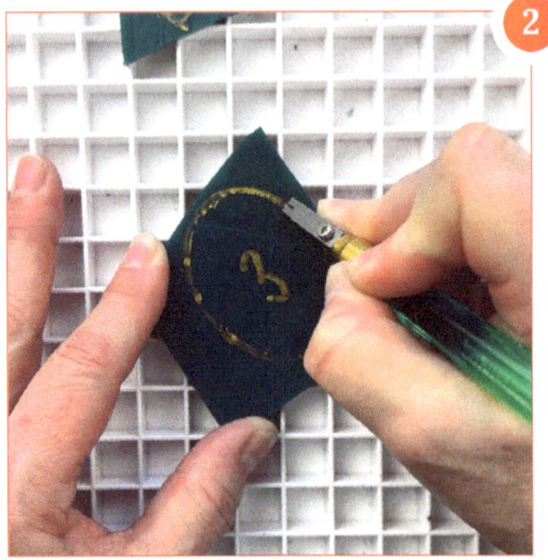

2 Score your glass

Use the glass cutter to score your piece inside the marker line and as close as possible to the pattern. You'll be able to grind excess glass for a precise fit later.

Touch the cutter firmly to the glass, and maintain steady pressure as you push or pull the cutter across the glass from edge to edge. When done properly, you will hear the glass "sing."

- ▸ **For straight lines:** Use a straight cutting edge as a guide and pull the cutter toward you.
- ▸ **For shapes and curves:** Push the cutter away from you.

It's important to never go over the same score line twice, as it will damage the cutting wheel and the glass may not break properly. If the score is not successful, you may need to shift your pattern to another area on the glass and try again.

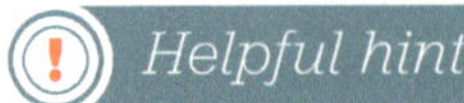

CUTTING STEEP CURVES

Shaping curved pieces may take a little extra work. To create steep curves, slowly score and break away the area with a series of shallow curves. The diagrams here show the best way to achieve this.

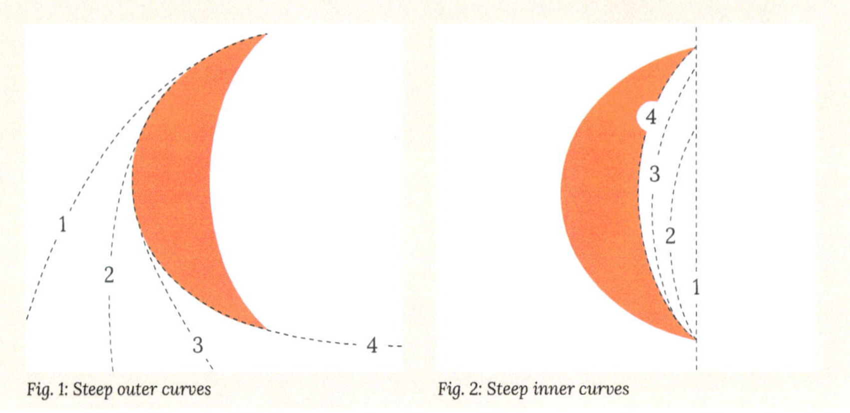

Fig. 1: Steep outer curves   Fig. 2: Steep inner curves

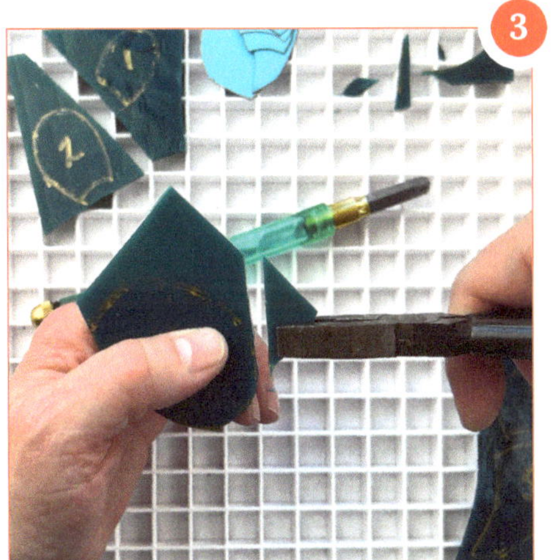

③ *Break your glass along the score line*

Grasp the glass on each side of the score line and, with steady pressure, fold your hands down to snap it apart. For small or difficult-to-hold pieces, use grozier pliers to hold the glass on one or both sides. For straight lines, use running pliers.

Break each cut after scoring. The glass surface can heal quickly after scoring, so the longer you wait, the harder it is to get a clean break.

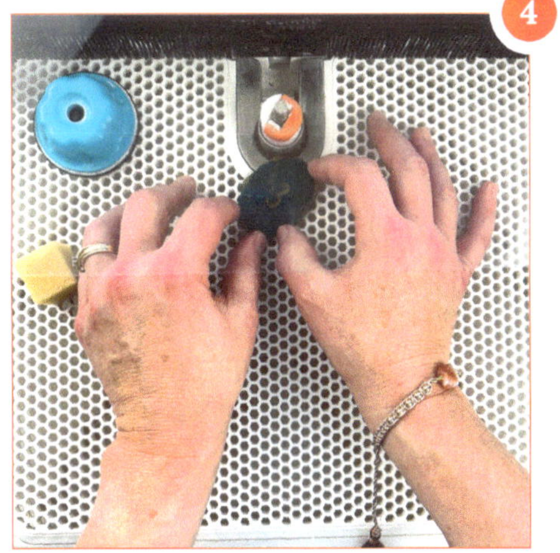

④ *Shape your glass*

Turn on your grinder and gently but firmly push your piece against the bit to knock off any glass that falls outside your pattern lines.

Grind as closely as possible to the pattern line, so your pieces will fit tightly and more accurately.

The edges of your glass may chip during the grinding process. Occasionally, large chips happen. Check your glass after grinding to be sure any chips can be covered by foil. If not, grind a little bit of the chipped edge away until it can be covered.

If the pattern lines were lost during handling and are no longer visible, simply retrace your pattern over the cut glass piece to refresh your boundaries.

 *Helpful hint*

ROUGH AND READY

Even if you have a perfect cut, it's still a good idea to run the perimeter of your piece across the grinder bit. This adds texture to the surface for better foil adhesion.

Foiling

▸ 7/32" black-backed copper foil tape ▸ Fid ▸ Precision craft knife
▸ Rubbing alcohol ▸ Paper towels

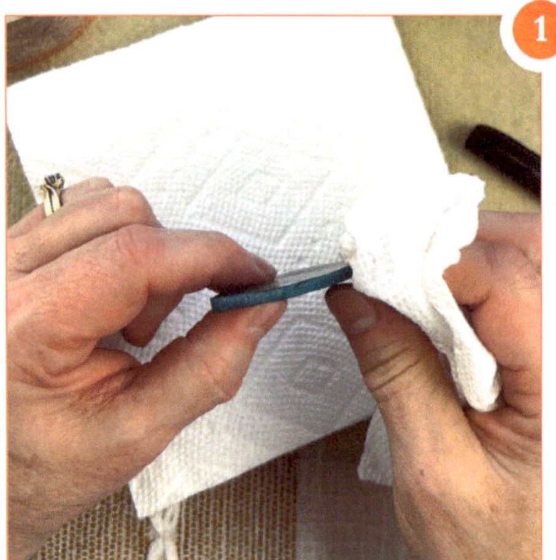

① Clean each piece

Use a paper towel to clean each piece with rubbing alcohol. This removes cutting oil and residue from grinding, which helps the foil adhere to the edge of the glass.

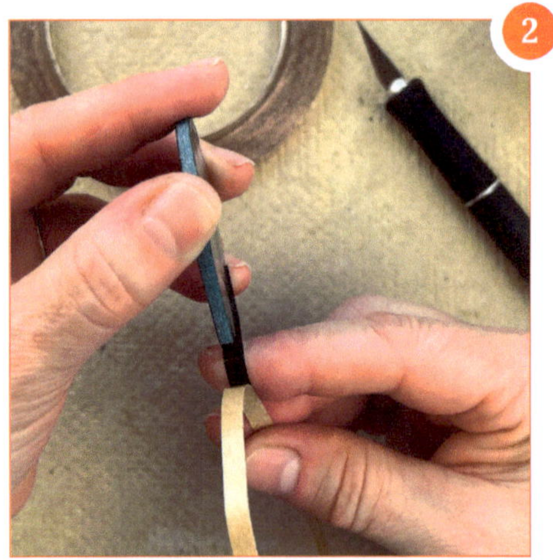

② Apply foil

Peel a small amount of the paper backing from the start of the foil tape, and center the adhesive side of the foil on the edge of the glass. Begin on an interior edge that will not be located along the outer edge of the assembled suncatcher. Continue to wrap around the perimeter of the glass. Slowly peel away the backing as you work. Continue around the piece until foil has been applied along the entire edge, overlapping itself by approximately 1/4".

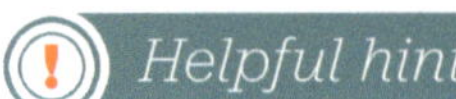

ⓘ *Helpful hint*

ROCK THE CURVE

When foiling inner curves, take your time and slowly rock your fid along the foil on the curve while gently pushing down — kind of like "stretching" the foil. This prevents the foil from splitting. Solder flows along the foil lines, so if there is a gap in the foil, there will be a gap in the solder.

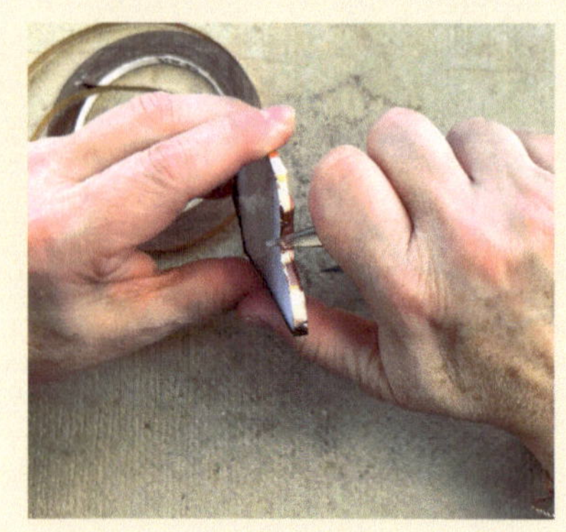

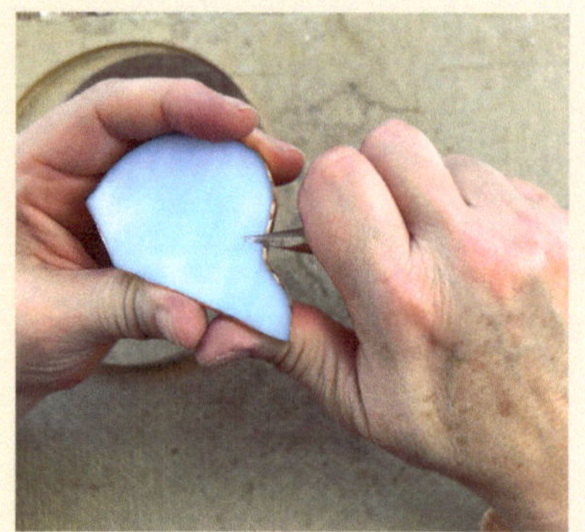

Stained Glass Suncatchers

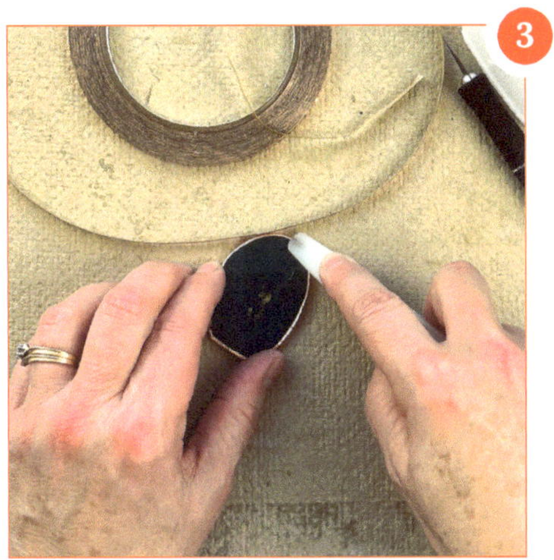

3 *Burnish the foil*

Use your fid to gently burnish (press down and smooth) the foil along the edge and over the sides, so that the foil is firmly adhered to the glass. After burnishing all edges, use the fid or your fingernail to fold the corners down.

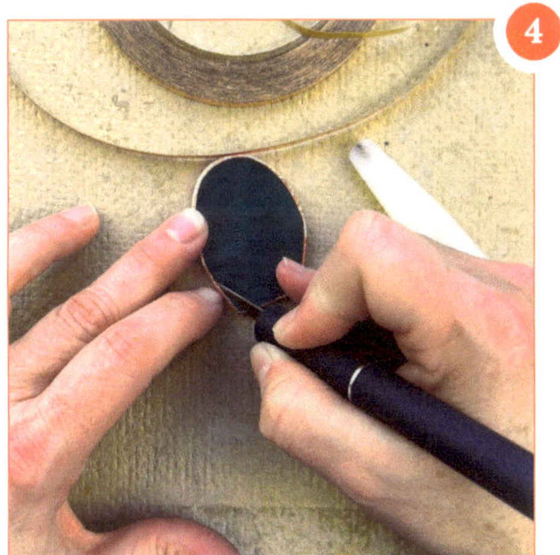

4 *Trim the foil*

Use a precision craft knife to trim any edges or seams that don't quite match up. Solder will follow the foil, so it should be as smooth as possible to keep it flowing in a nice, neat line.

Helpful hint (!)

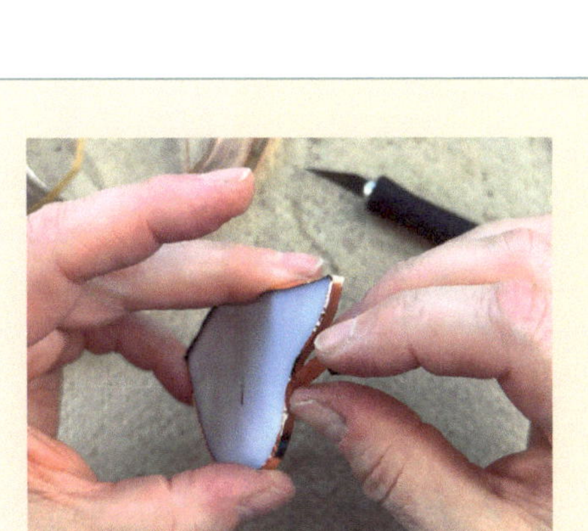

REPAIRING SPLITS

You can repair a split before soldering by cutting a small piece of foil to bridge the gap, allowing about 1/4" on either side. Reapply this over the existing foil. Then burnish and trim so that it meets up properly. There is a risk of the newly applied foil coming loose, so use flux sparingly and carefully when soldering that area. If it's in an intricate spot or on a textured piece of glass, it's sometimes best to re-foil the entire piece.

Soldering and wiring

Supplies

▸ Pattern ▸ 60/40 solid core solder ▸ Soldering iron stand

▸ Soldering iron with temperature control ▸ Brass sponge with holder

▸ Sal ammoniac block ▸ Liquid stained glass flux ▸ Flux brush (acid brush)

▸ Aluminum push pins ▸ 20-gauge pre-tinned copper wire

▸ 2 pairs of needle-nose pliers ▸ Wire cutters

▸ Heat-resistant soldering surface ▸ Metal O-ring

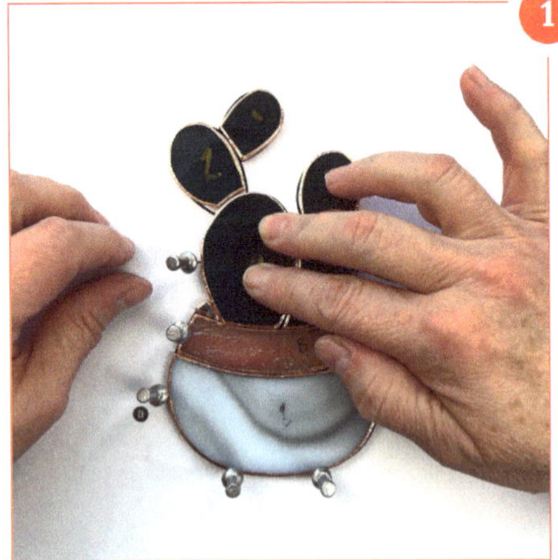

1 *Position your foiled pieces*

Place your working layout copy of the pattern on your heat-resistant soldering surface. Then place each foiled piece of glass on top of the corresponding number, so that it is in its final, correct position on the pattern. Once all pieces are placed, secure the perimeter with aluminum push pins to keep all pieces together while soldering.

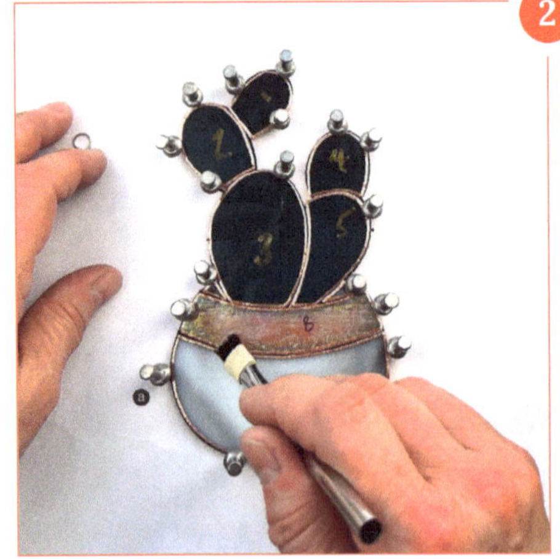

2 *Apply flux*

With a flux brush, apply a moderate amount of liquid flux to the section of foil you are going to solder, working on one small area at a time. Too much flux will make the solder sputter. If you do not have enough flux, your solder will become stuck and will not flow.

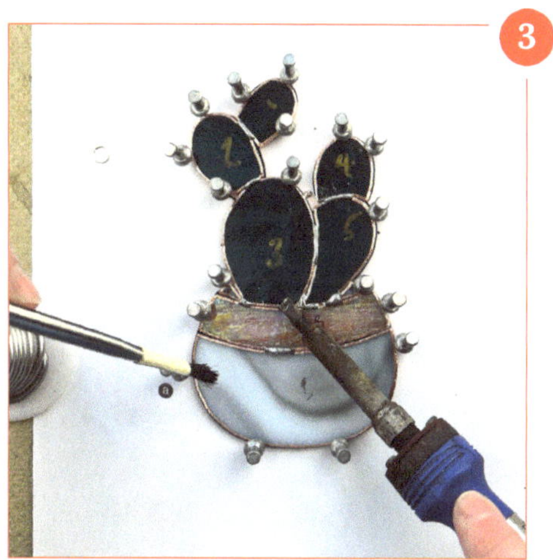

③ *Tack solder*

After you apply flux, melt a small amount of solder onto the tip of your heated iron and apply it to each joint and along the seams in approximately 1" intervals. This will hold the pieces in place as you continue to work. When all pieces are attached, remove the aluminum push pins from around the perimeter.

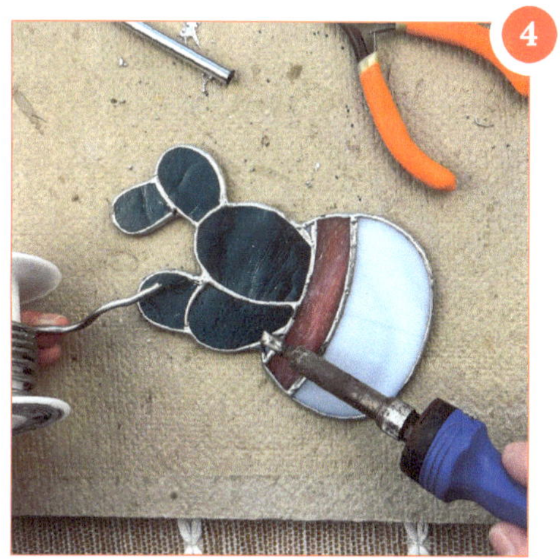

④ *Flat solder*

Working in sections, apply flux. Then cover all seams with an even, flat line of solder. This doesn't have to be perfect — it's a base layer that holds the piece together and helps stop drip-through when applying your finish bead.

Turn the flat-soldered piece over, and repeat the process on the back.

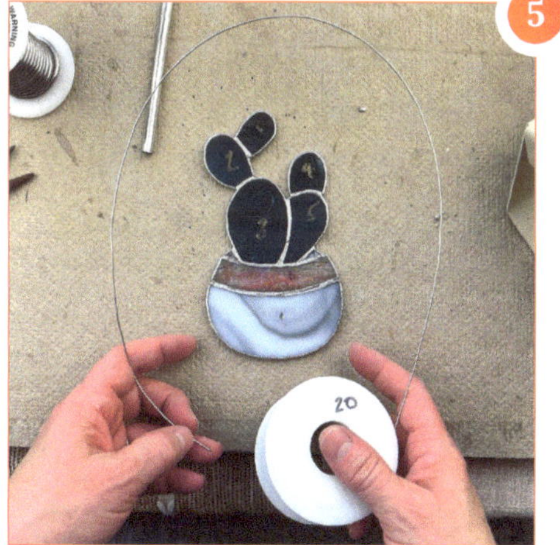

⑤ *Prepare your wire*

Estimate and cut the amount of wire to fit the entire perimeter of the suncatcher.

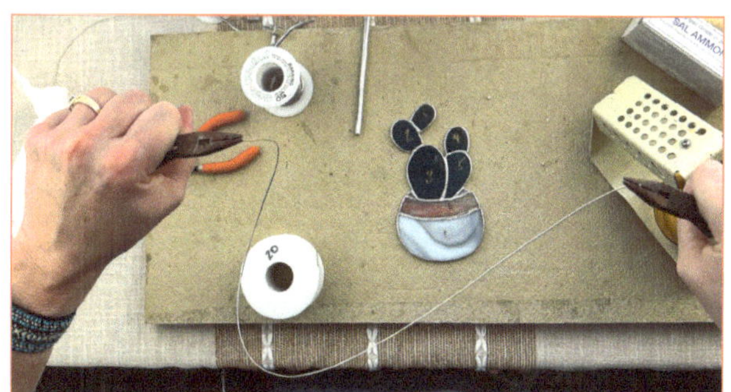

Straighten 20-gauge pre-tinned copper wire using two pairs of needle-nose pliers. Grip the pliers firmly and tug the wire horizontally a few times until the wire is smooth.

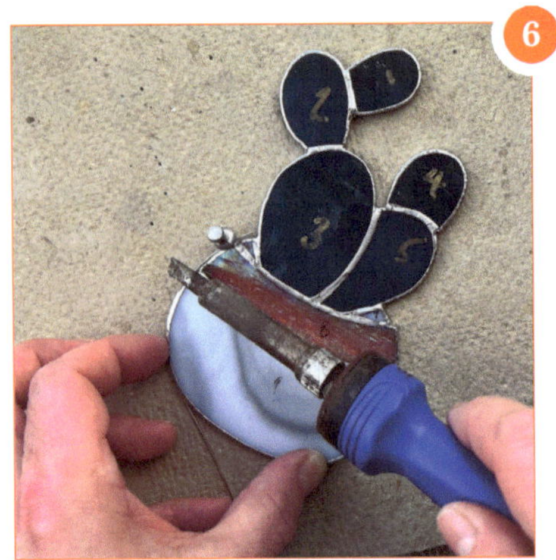

6 ### *Wire your suncatcher*

Wiring the outer perimeter of your suncatcher adds support and longevity to the final piece.

To provide a smooth surface to attach the wire, work around the perimeter to melt off any excess solder that may have dripped over the edge when flat soldering.

Start wiring in a joint for stability. In approximately 1" intervals, apply flux then use a small amount of solder to tack the wire to the center of the edge of the glass. Follow the perimeter around corners and curves. If needed, use needle-nose pliers to hold the wire in place. End in the same joint you started and cut off any excess wire.

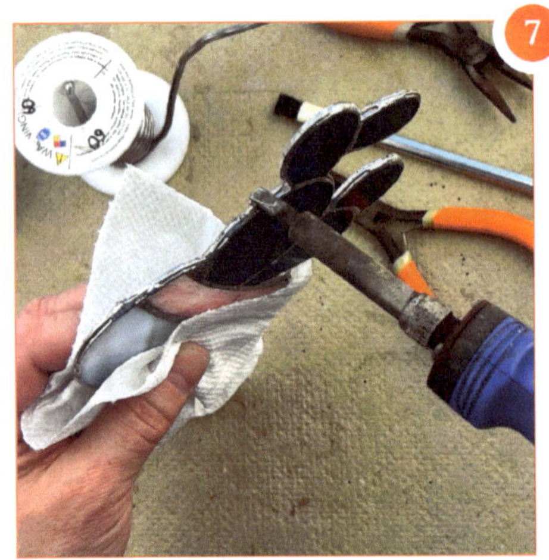

7 ### *Solder the perimeter*

Slowly apply a rounded bead around your perimeter. Working in small increments, place your iron tip on the glass edge and allow the solder to pool. Lift your iron away from the solder for about 10 seconds to allow it to set before moving on to the next section. Rotate the suncatcher as needed so that the area you are soldering remains as level as possible.

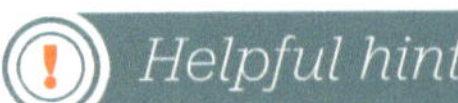

(!) *Helpful hint*

KEEP YOUR IRON TIP CLEAN

Use your brass sponge to remove residual solder from your tip while working. After each soldering session, re-tin your tip with sal ammoniac. This helps maintain the life of the tip.

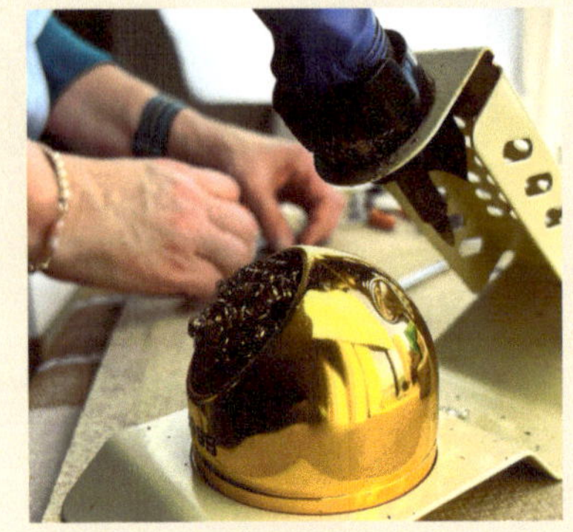

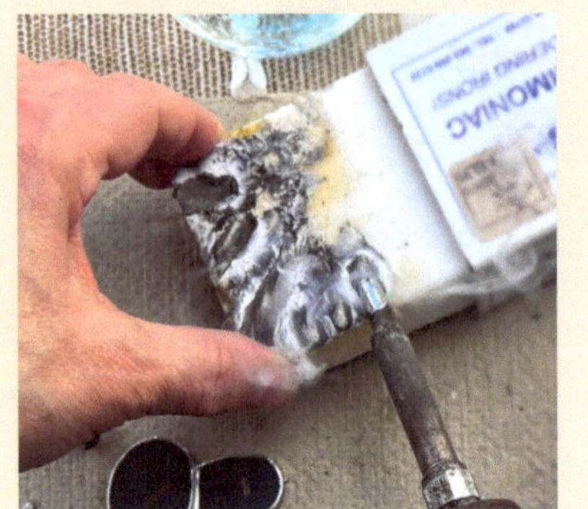

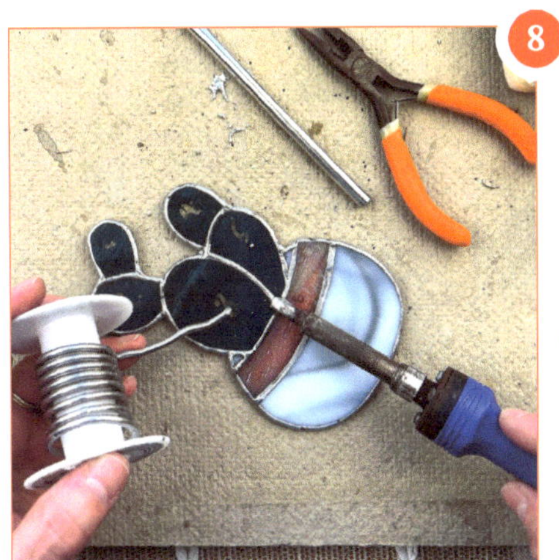

8 *Finish soldering*

A finish bead is a smooth, rounded layer of solder on the surface of each seam that is approximately as tall as it is wide. Apply flux and work slowly and evenly to solder a finish bead on the back of your suncatcher. Turn it over and repeat the process on the front.

! Helpful hints

SMOOTH JOINTS

To smooth your soldered joints, place the iron on the joint, allow for a full melt (count to 3!), and then lift your iron straight up. Practice makes perfect with this technique.

KEEP IT COOL

Be mindful of the amount of time spent in one area — if the glass gets too hot, it can crack. Move on to a different section and let the glass cool before coming back to it.

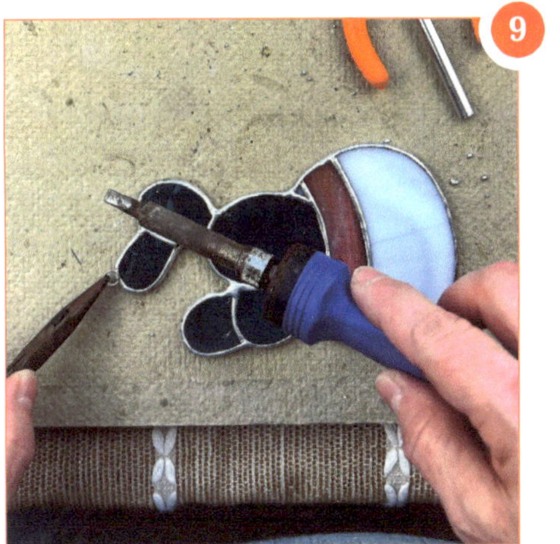

9 *Attach the O-ring*

Place the O-ring in a spot that is optimal for hanging. Think of the angle at which you'd like your suncatcher to hang. Be mindful of the center of balance — it's not always the center of the project. Attach the O-ring to the outside perimeter of your suncatcher with solder.

Note: Large suncatchers can be heavy and may require two O-rings to evenly distribute the weight when hanging.

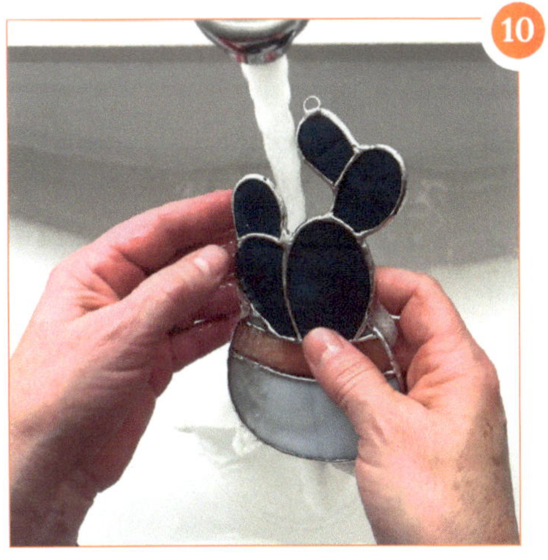

10 *Clean your suncatcher*

Rinse your suncatcher with water only to clean off the flux. If the suncatcher is still warm from soldering, use warm water to avoid a sudden and drastic change in temperature that may cause the glass to crack.

Finishing

▸ Medium (grade 00) steel wool ▸ Patina (black for solder/lead)

▸ Stained glass finishing compound ▸ Soft-bristled brush (shoeshine brush)

▸ Gloves ▸ Rag for polishing ▸ Fishing line or chain for hanging

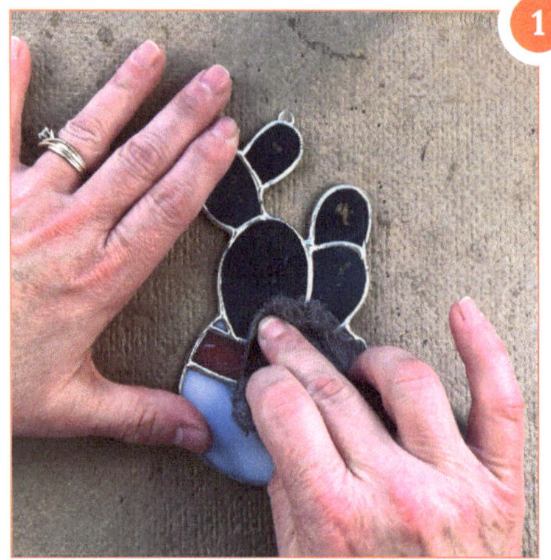

1 Prepare your solder for patina

Use steel wool to clean your glass and add texture to your solder. This helps the patina adhere to the solder lines.

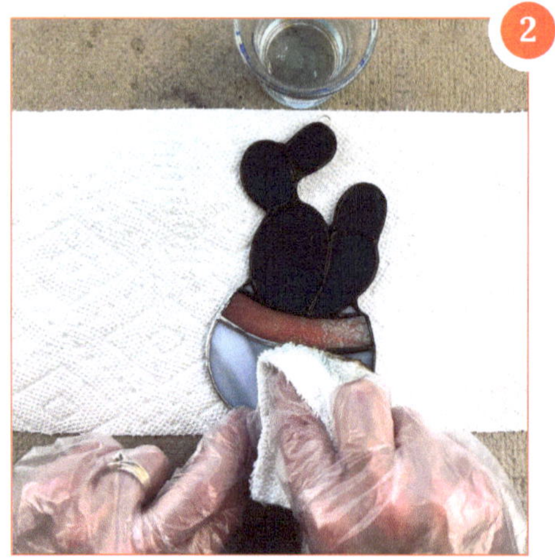

2 Apply patina

Wearing gloves, use a rag to evenly apply patina along the solder lines. Absorb any extra patina on the glass with a paper towel. Patina can damage glass if left on too long. Allow the patina to set for 20-30 minutes, then promptly rinse well with water and pat dry. Allow the suncatcher to dry thoroughly before polishing.

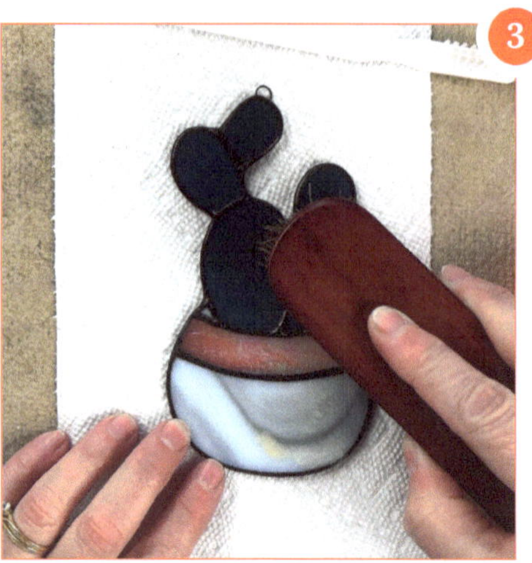

3 Polish and hang

Apply stained glass finishing compound with a soft-bristled brush to polish your finished project. Allow it to dry to a haze, then buff with a soft cloth. You can easily remove polish from nooks and crannies using a toothbrush.

Attach fishing line or chain to the O-ring to hang.

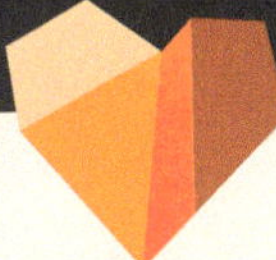

Congratulations!

You made a stained glass suncatcher! Hang your masterpiece in a bright space to enjoy the full beauty of the glass. The skills you've learned throughout this process are a great foundation for any stained glass project, so keep practicing!

When you've finished your project, share a photo and tag us on social media: **@glassclasspatterns**

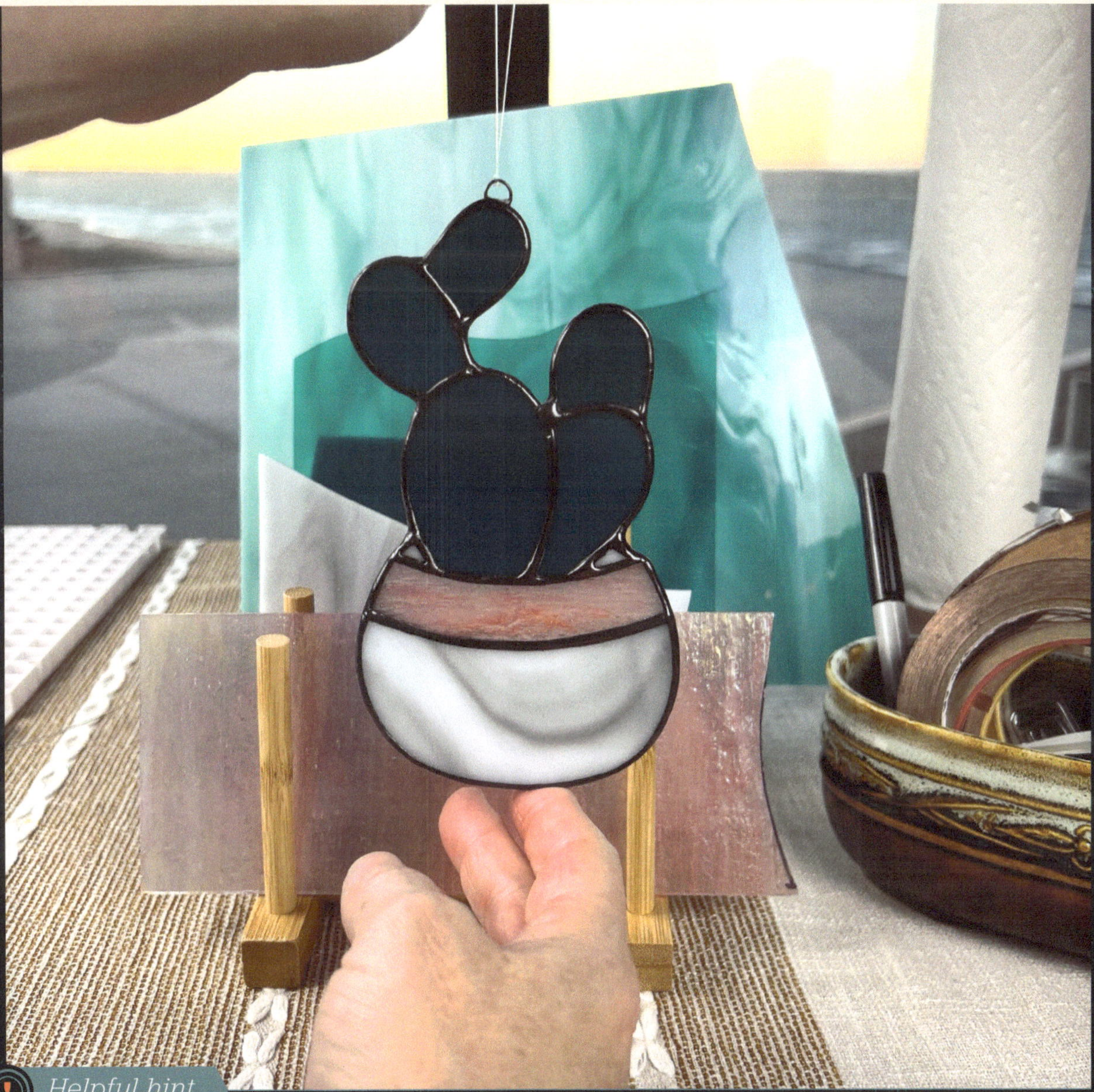

CARING FOR YOUR SUNCATCHER

If your suncatcher needs to be cleaned or brightened up, simply spray with a non-ammonia formula glass cleaner and dry with a paper towel. You can also use warm, soapy water and rinse thoroughly on each side.

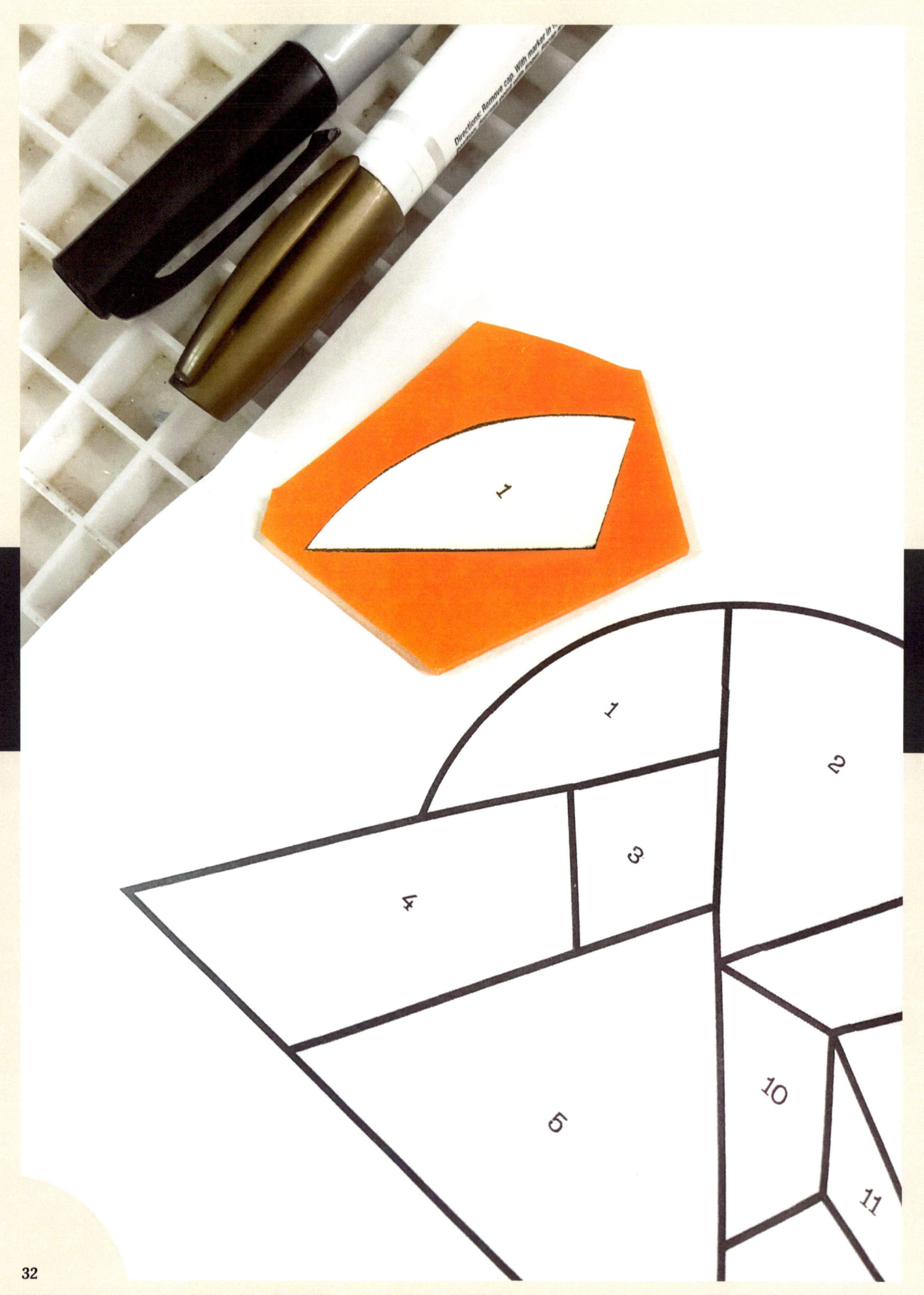

1
1
2
3
4
10
5
11

3 *Patterns*

It's time to put the cutter to the glass and start making. We've provided an at-a-glance key for each pattern to give you an overview of the total number of pieces, size of the finished suncatcher, and level of difficulty. Think of each pattern as a blueprint to help you bring your vision to life.

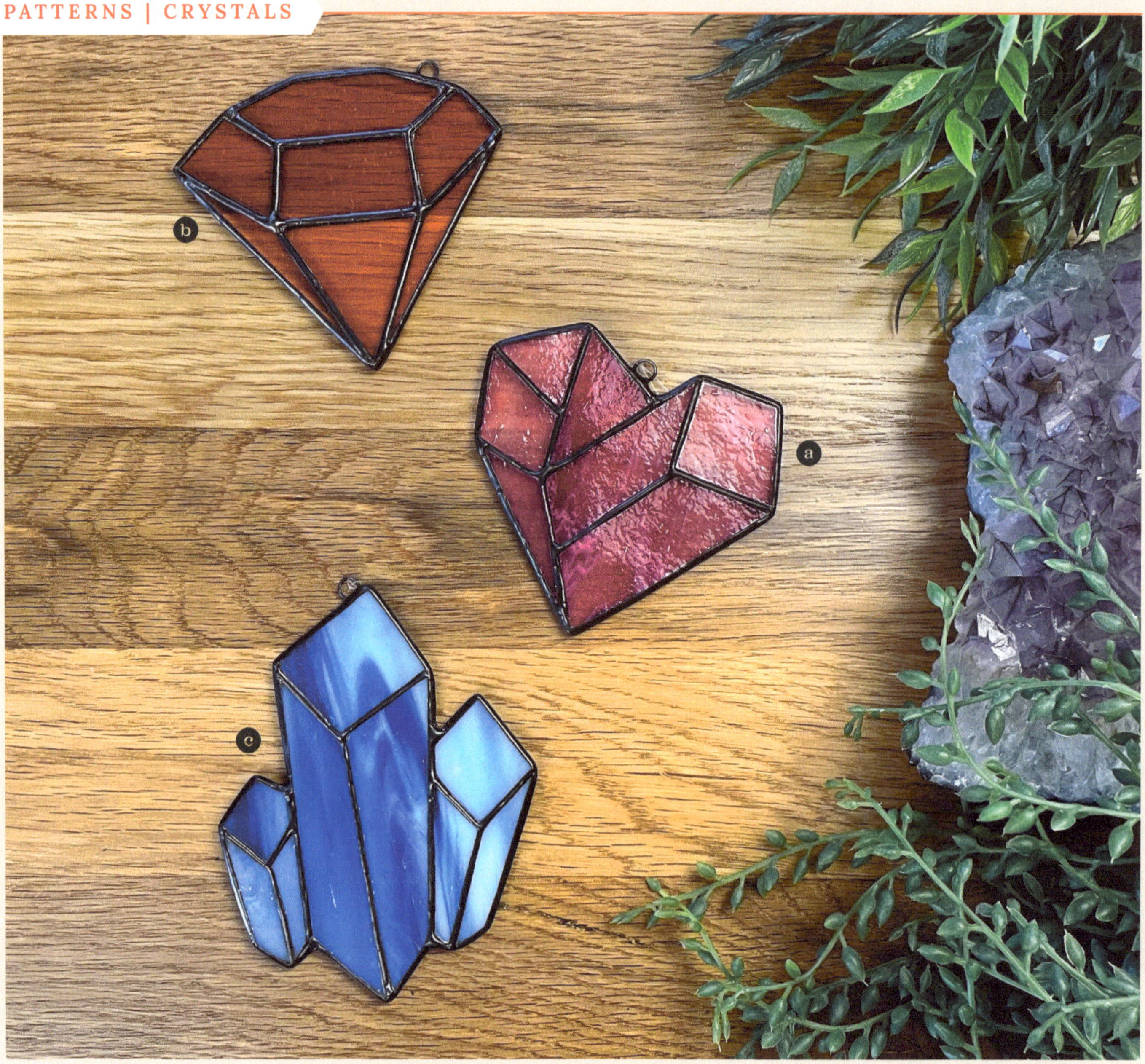

About these patterns

Crystals are widely embraced as conduits for healing and restorative energy. With their geometric shapes and clean lines, each unique crystal and stone represents an intention that you can translate into your suncatcher for yourself or to share with others.

Heidi's tips

Be wary of heavily textured glass for straight lines. It can soften the edges, which can distort clean cuts.

Research what different crystals and stones represent, and choose your glass accordingly. For the sample suncatchers, the heart was made to replicate rose quartz, which represents love, warmth, and compassion. The gem's color nods to topaz, a symbol of passion and purpose. For the cluster, we channeled blue fluorite to signify clarity, trust, and calm energy.

TOTAL NUMBER OF PIECES

a 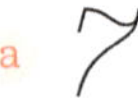 7

b 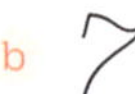 7 c 9

FINISHED SIZES (approx.)

a 3.6" x 3.6"

b 3.7" x 3.5" c 3.6" x 4.5"

LEVEL OF DIFFICULTY

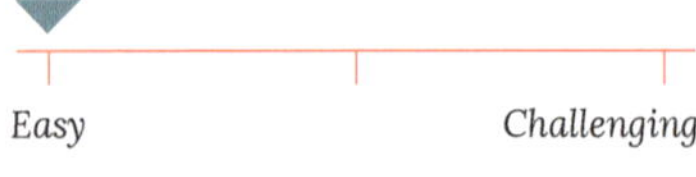

Easy   Challenging

Stained Glass Suncatchers

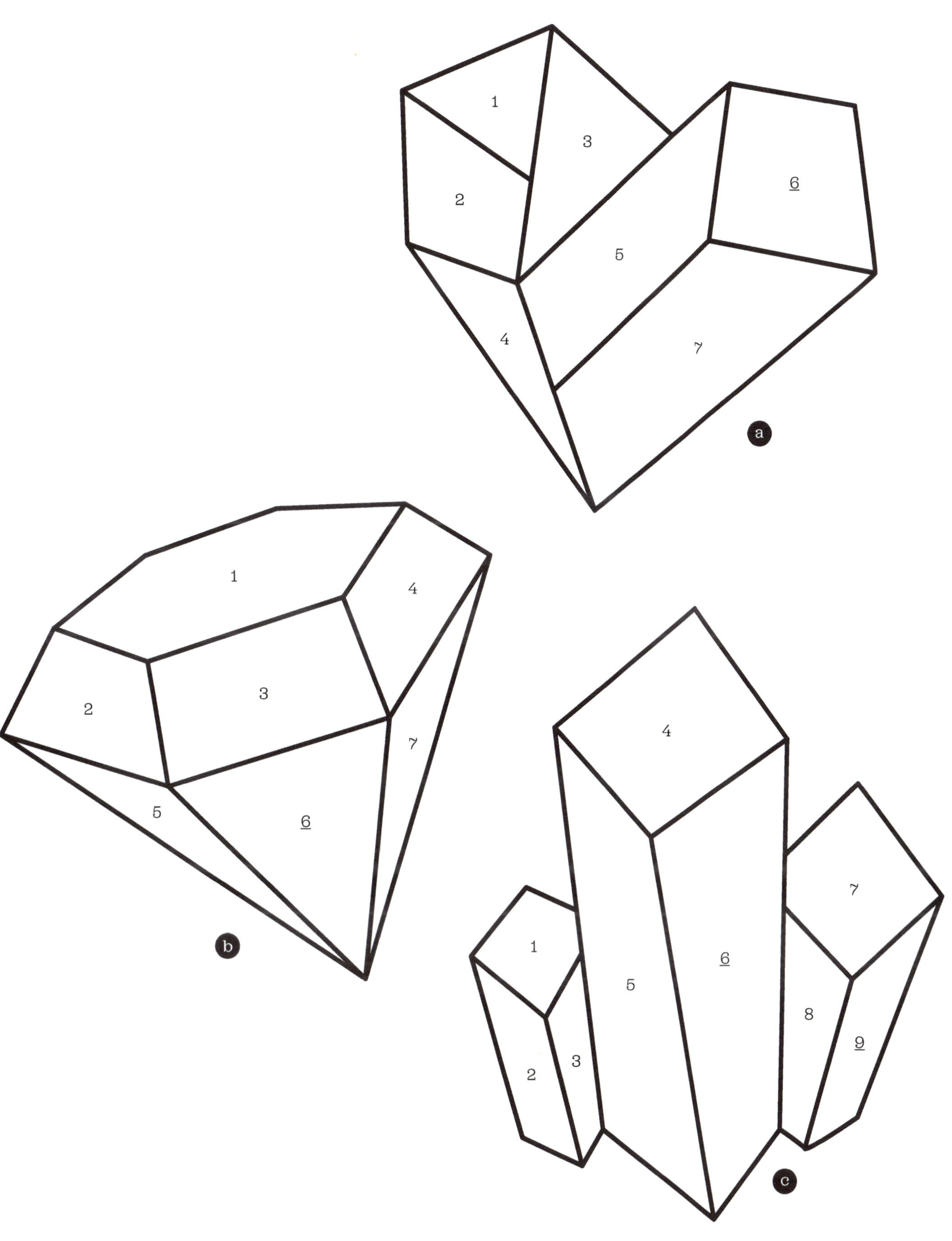

Crystals

© 2022 Glass Class. All rights reserved. | glassclasspatterns.com

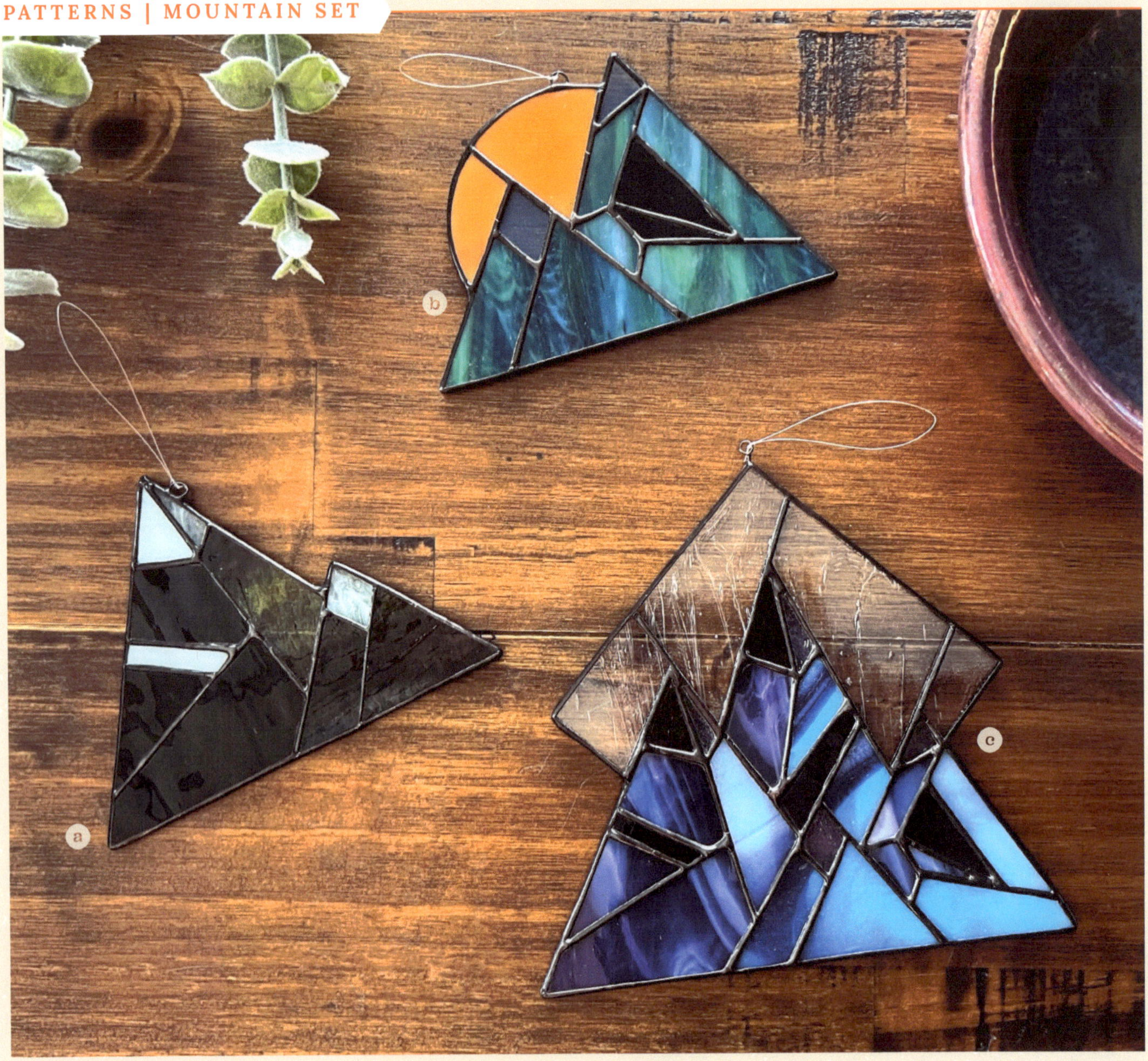

About these patterns

This series was inspired by a family trip to the Great Smoky Mountains. As we watched the sun set over the mountains from the porch of our log cabin rental, our family played guitar and sang along to the choruses of our favorite songs. We hope that this set evokes the same feelings of peace and perspective we felt that evening.

 Heidi's tips

Pull out a small portion of a larger pattern to create your own suncatcher.

Different color palettes can suggest different geographical locations.

TOTAL NUMBER OF PIECES

a *10*

b *12*   c *27*

FINISHED SIZES (approx.)

a *6" x 4.4"*

b *6" x 3.9"*   c *7.5" x 6.8"*

LEVEL OF DIFFICULTY

a,b c

Easy   Challenging

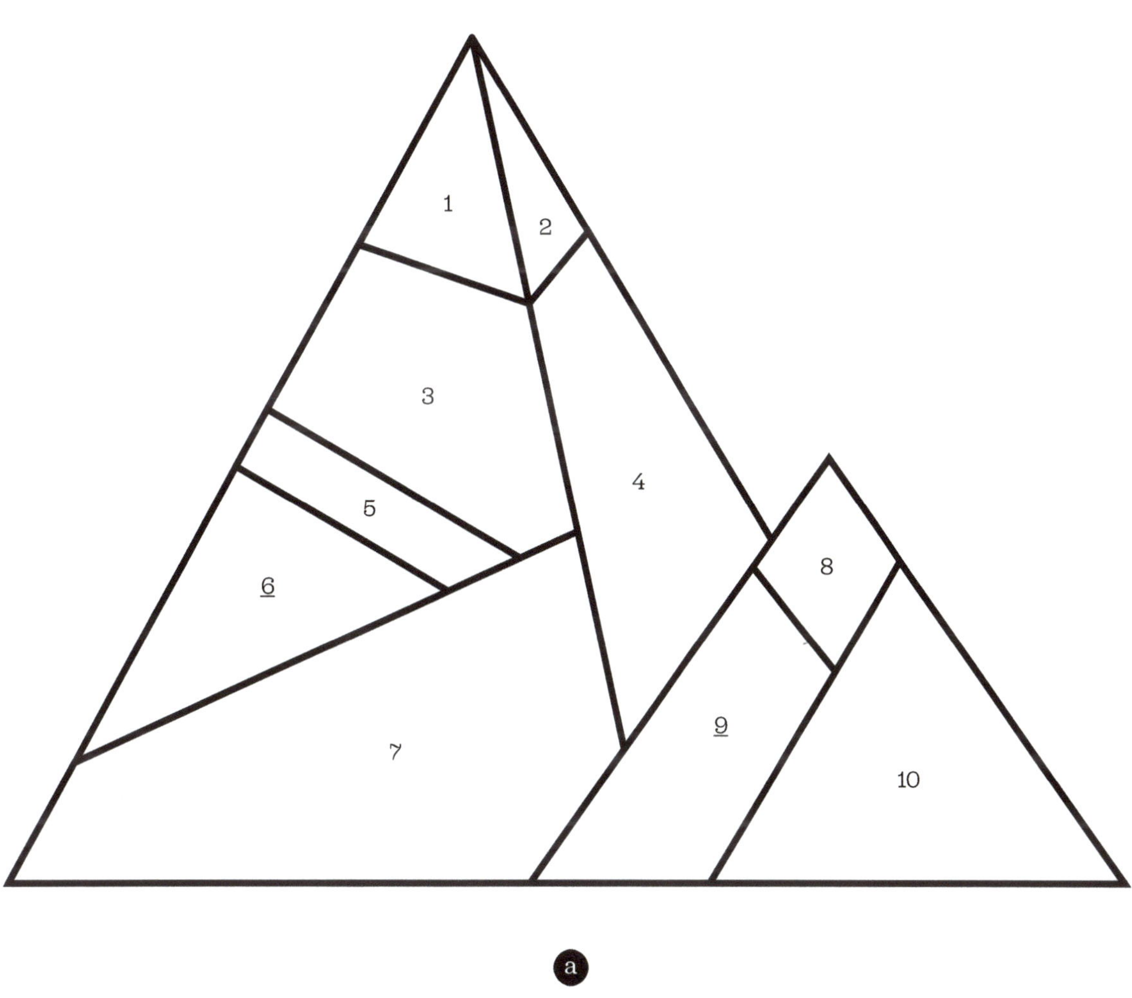

Simple mountains

© 2022 Glass Class. All rights reserved. | glassclasspatterns.com

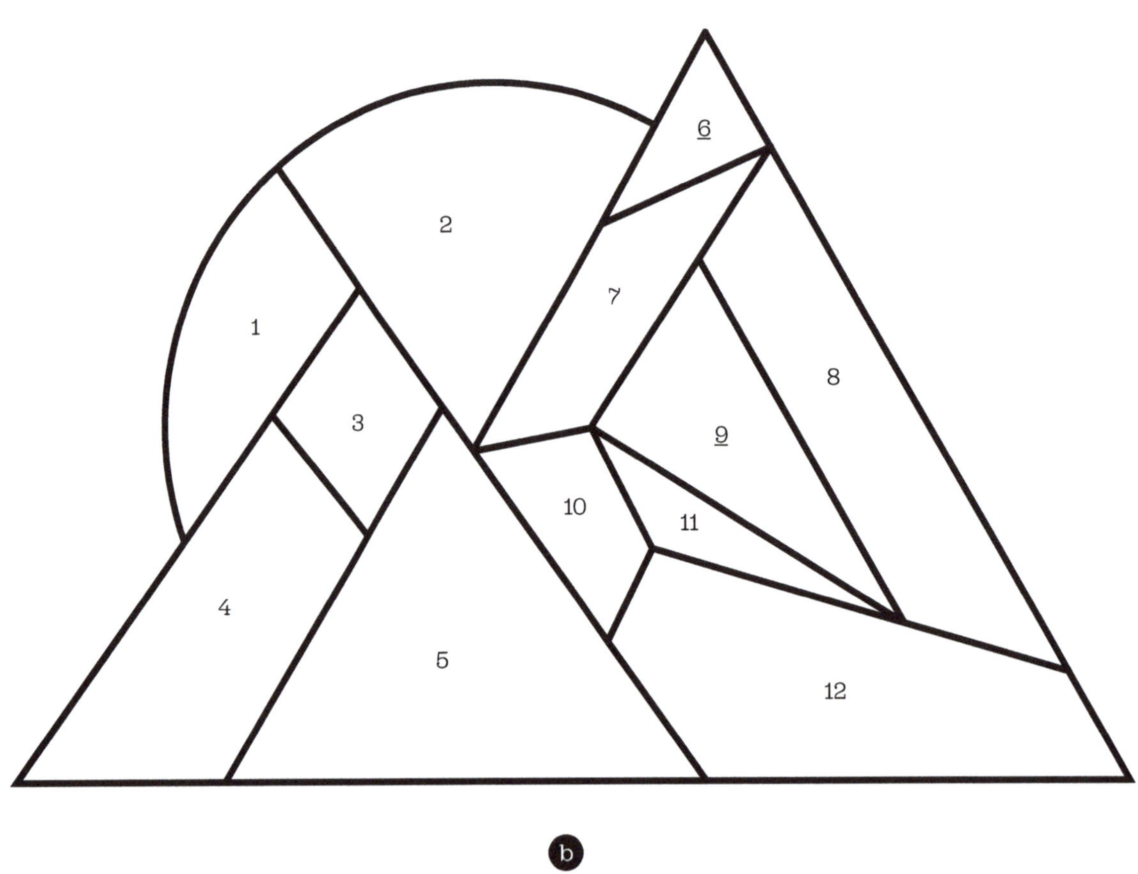

Mountains with sun

© 2022 Glass Class. All rights reserved. | glassclasspatterns.com

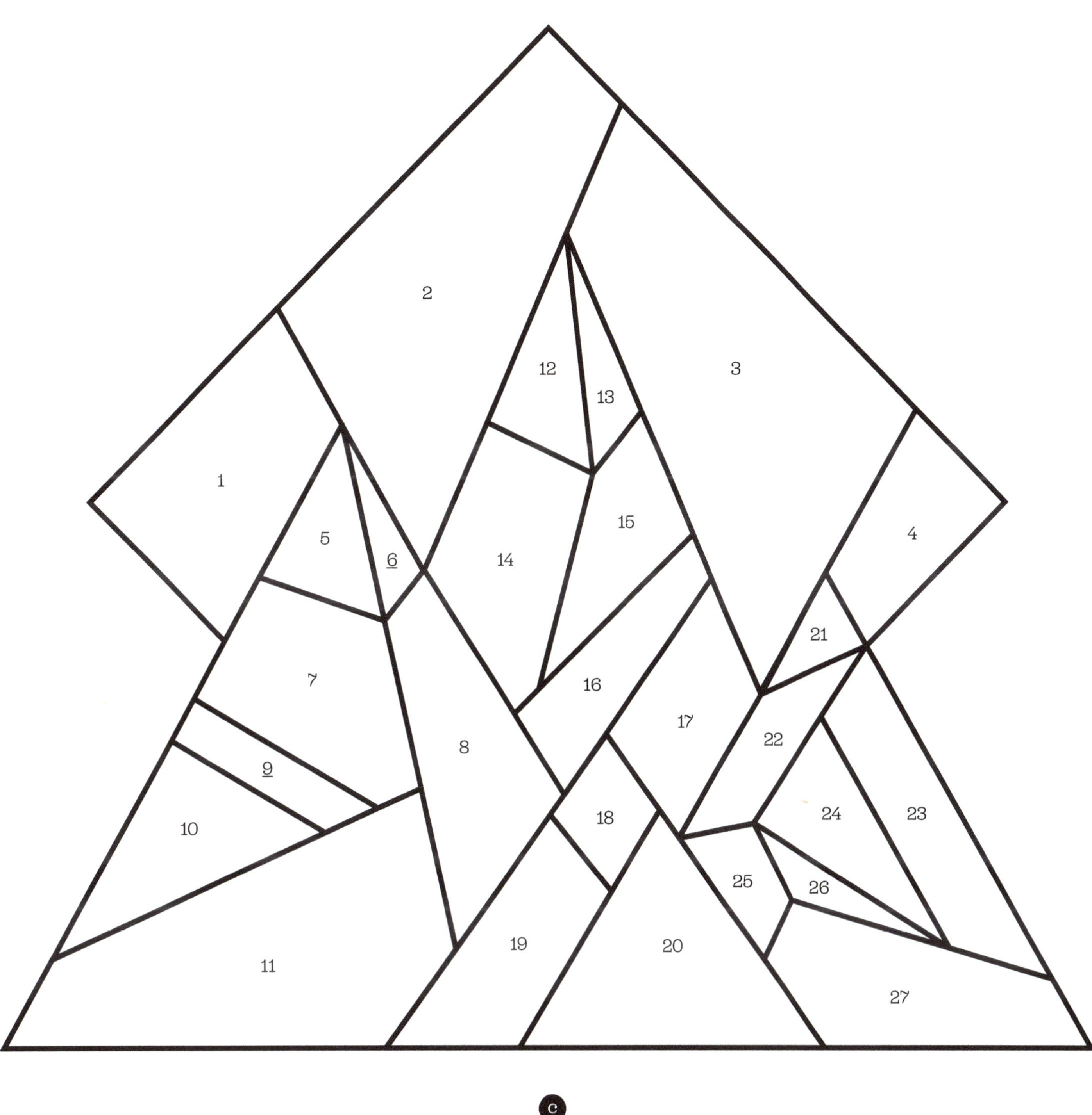

Mountain range

© 2022 Glass Class. All rights reserved. | glassclasspatterns.com

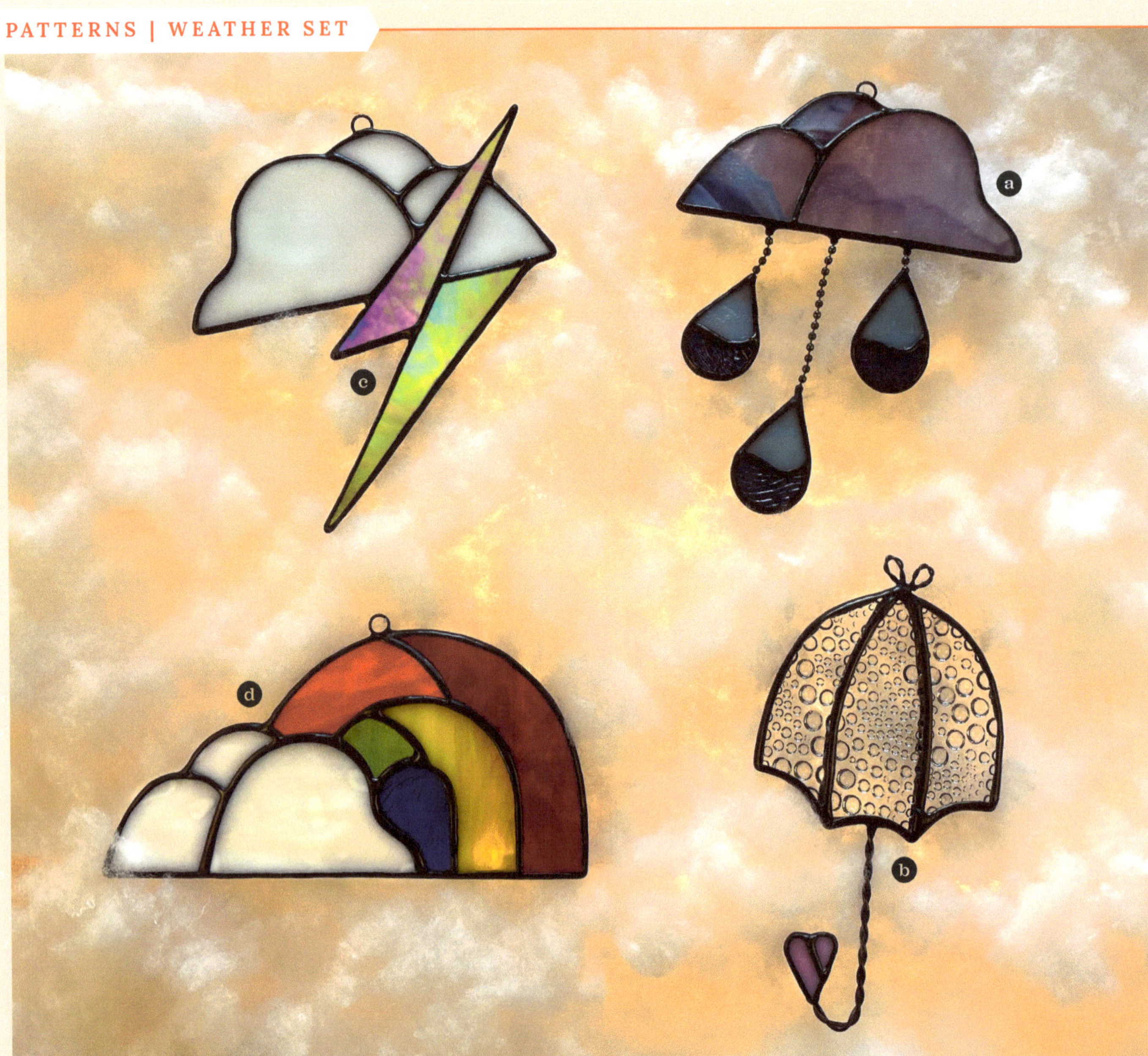

TOTAL NUMBER OF PIECES

a *9*   c *6*

b *5*   d *8*

FINISHED SIZES (approx.)

a *4.1" x 5.3"*   c *4.5" x 4.6"*

b *2.8" x 5.2"*   d *5.8" x 2.8"*

LEVEL OF DIFFICULTY

a,b c,d

Easy ——————— Challenging

About these patterns

This set gives "weather patterns" an entirely different meaning! Each pattern in this series can express a different feeling — a rainbow of hope, an umbrella for protection, a powerful lightning bolt, or serene raindrops.

Heidi's tips

Let your glass convey the weather. For example, use bright white clouds for sunny days or white/gray glass with blue undertones for cloudy days.

Be careful where you place the O-ring for hanging — crookedness is particularly apparent when your pattern has a flat bottom.

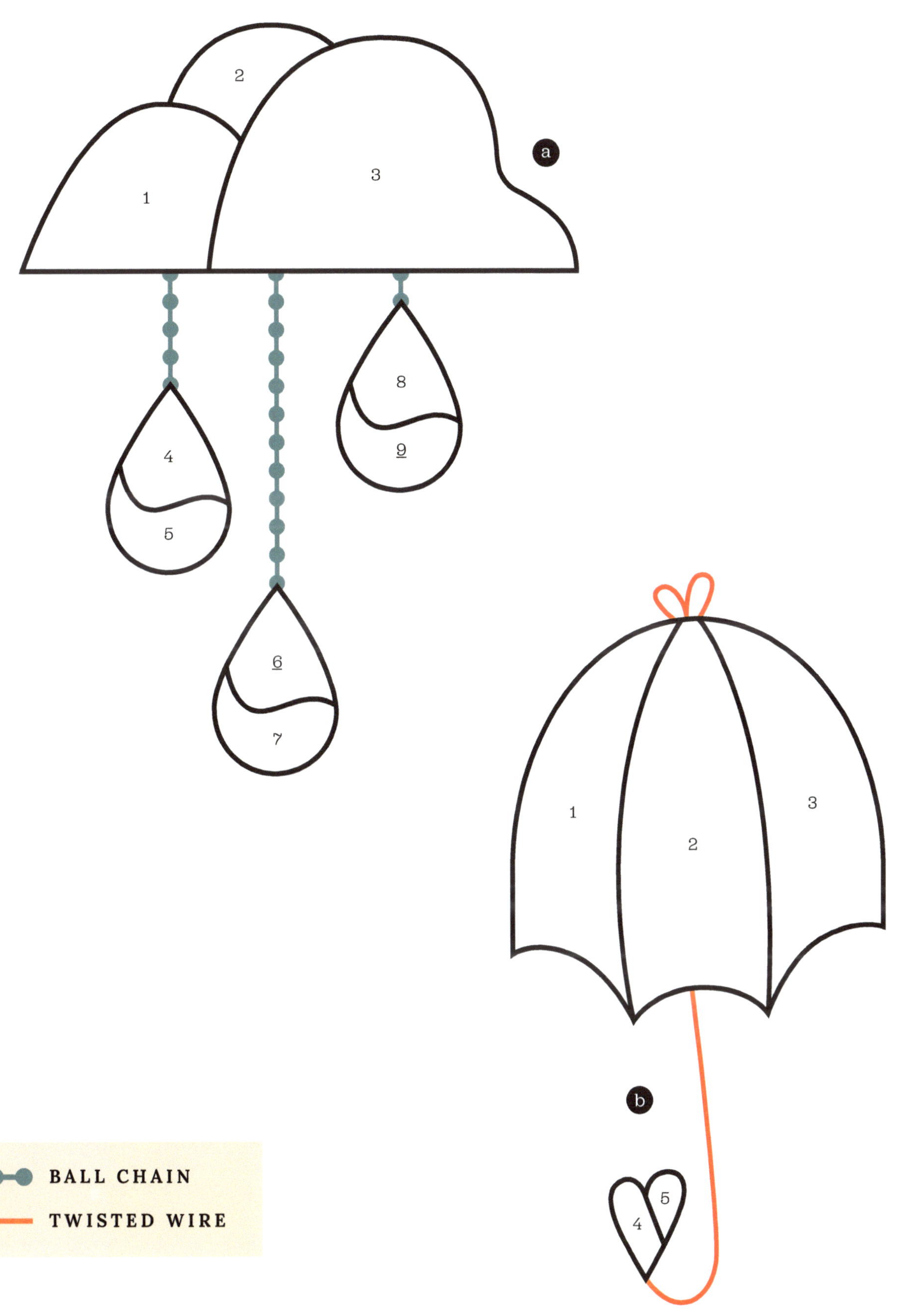

Raincloud & umbrella

© 2022 Glass Class. All rights reserved. | glassclasspatterns.com

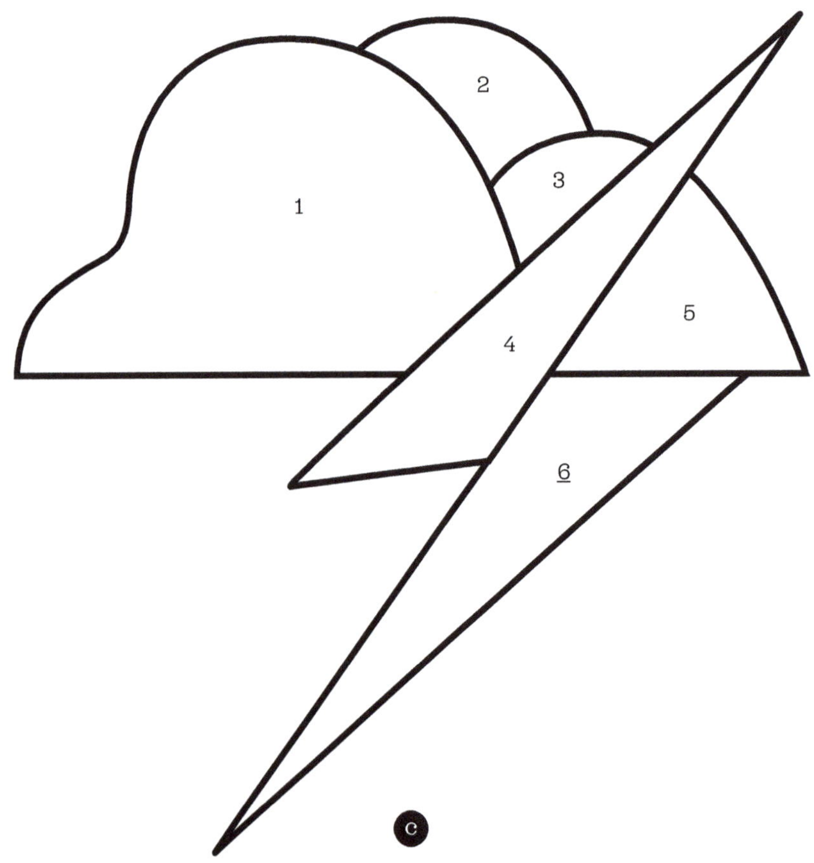

Thundercloud

© 2022 Glass Class. All rights reserved. | glassclasspatterns.com

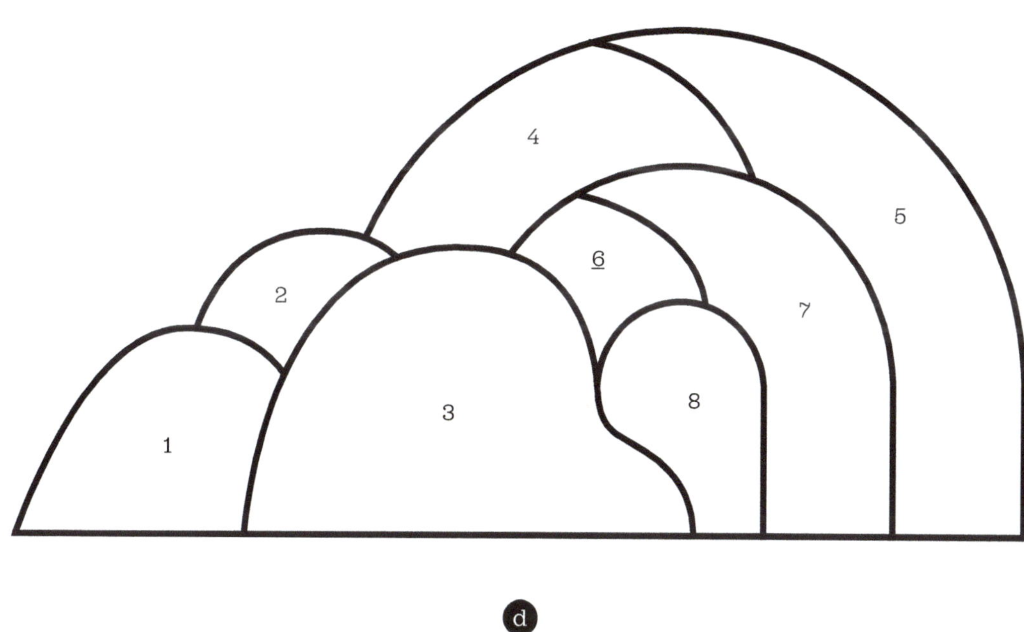

Rainbow

© 2022 Glass Class. All rights reserved. | glassclasspatterns.com

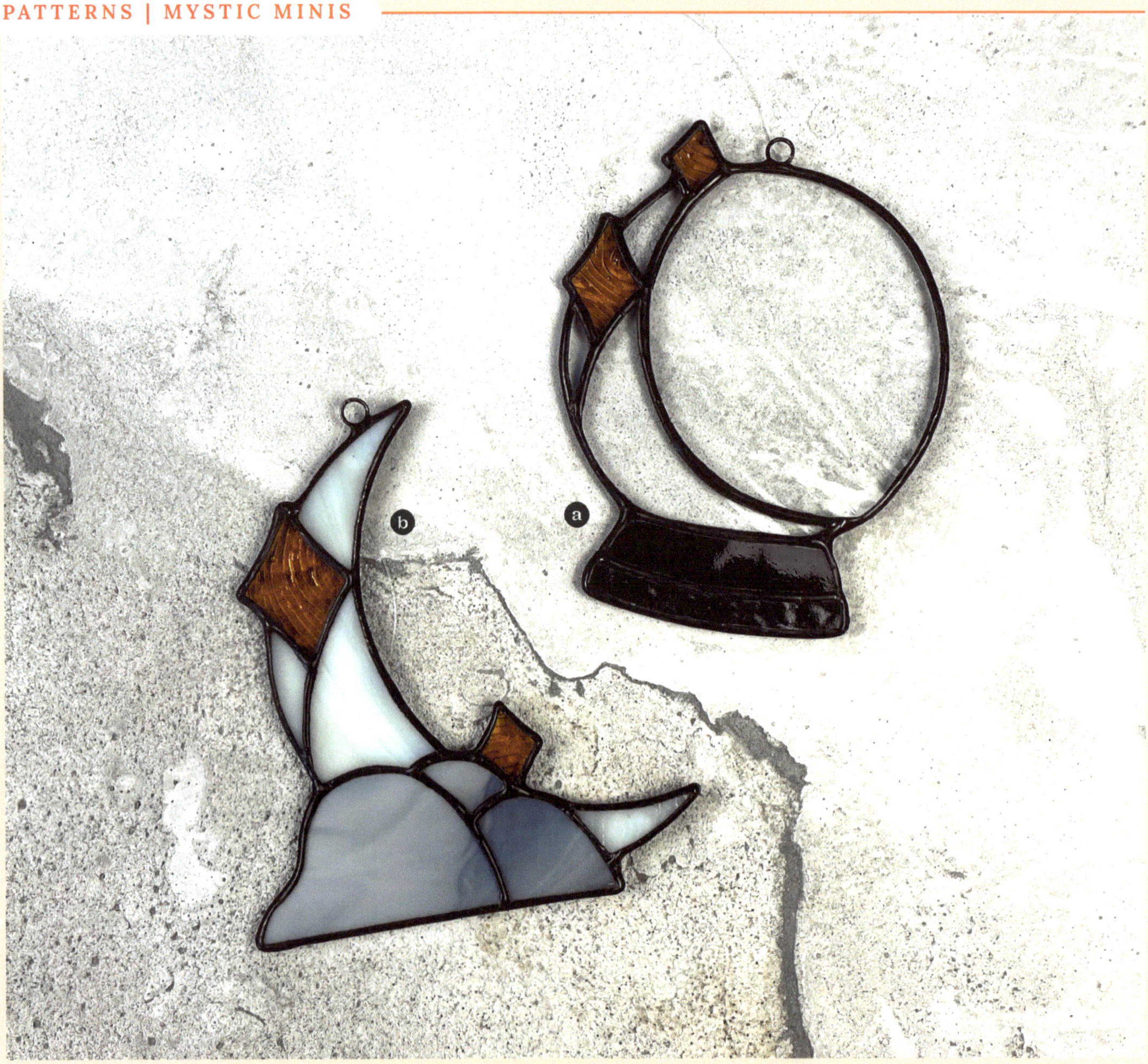

TOTAL NUMBER OF PIECES

a **8**   b **9**

FINISHED SIZES (approx.)

a *3.7" x 4.5"*

b *4.4" x 4.7"*

LEVEL OF DIFFICULTY

Easy ◀──────▶ Challenging

About these patterns

Our mystic mini set represents mystery, vision, and good fortune. Use moody or swirling glass to add intrigue to this pair. We predict these pieces will shine by the light of the sun or the glow of the moon.

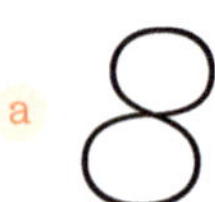 *Heidi's tips*

These patterns are relatively simple to wire, but adding a finish bead to the outside perimeter requires patience.

Solder in small increments while keeping that area level, and make sure to let your solder set before turning your piece.

Stained Glass Suncatchers

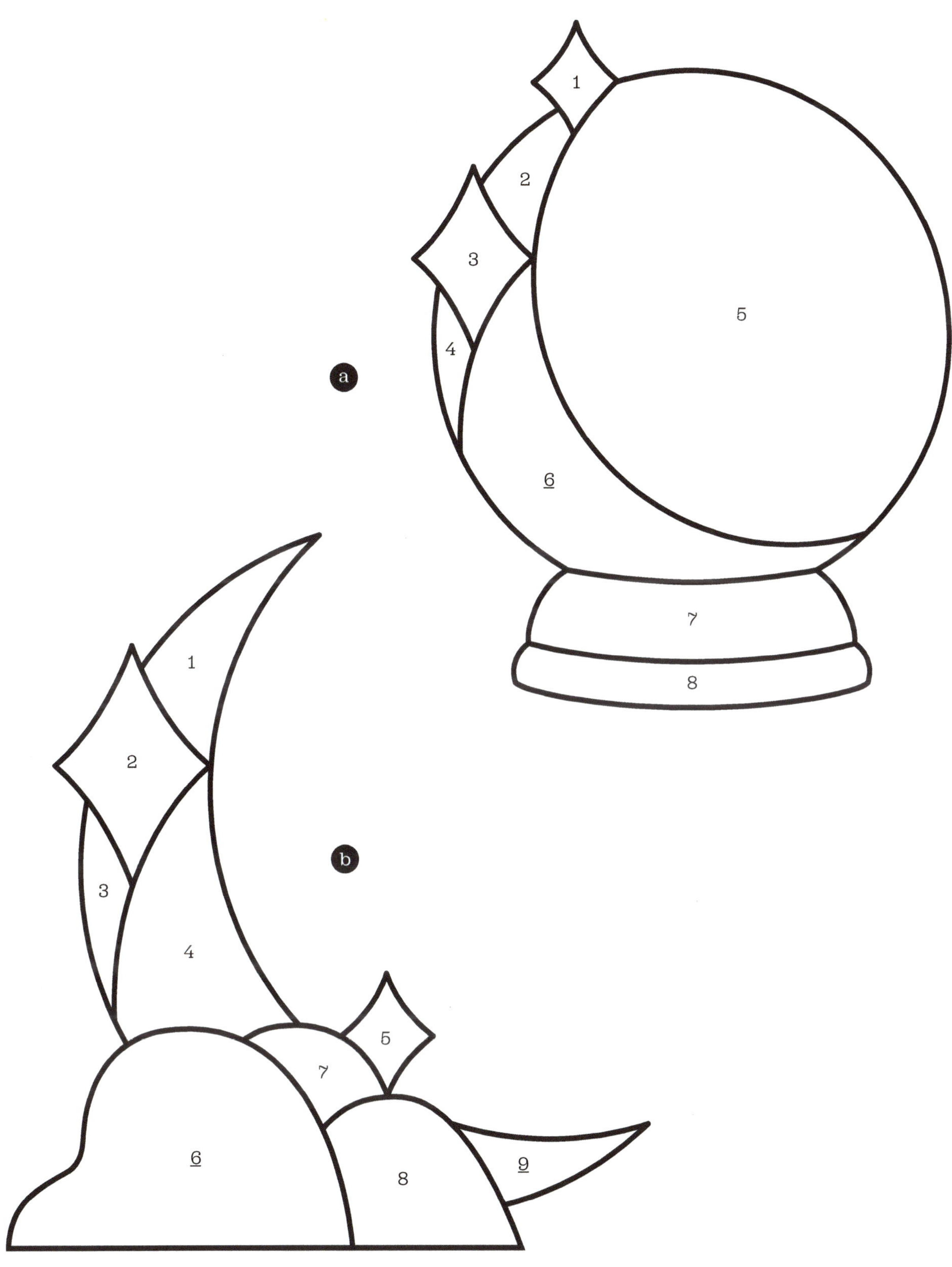

Mystic minis

© 2022 Glass Class. All rights reserved. | glassclasspatterns.com

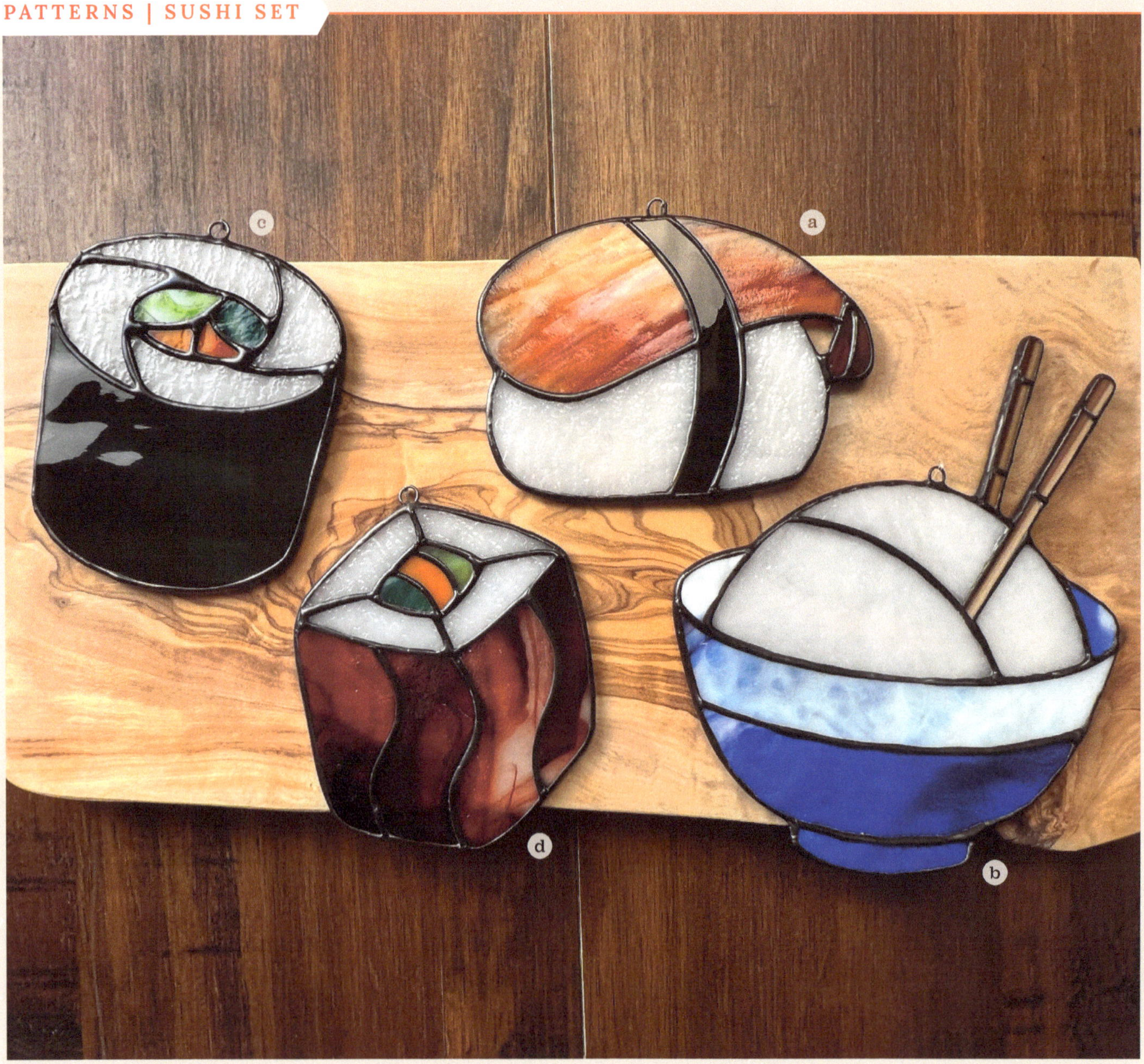

About these patterns

We were inspired by the bright colors, artfully crafted shapes, and delicious ingredients of sushi to create this series. The gifting and messaging options are endless for this trio — from "thank you soy much" to "you're on a roll!" With the bowl of rice on the side, you have the perfect set.

Heidi's tips

Glass choice is critical when representing something edible. Lifeless looking glass can appear unappetizing.

Use textured glass to represent fine details, like rice grains.

TOTAL NUMBER OF PIECES

a 7   c 9

b 14   d 11

FINISHED SIZES (approx.)

a 5" x 3.5"   c 3.5" x 4.2"

b 6" x 7"   d 3.6" x 4.2"

LEVEL OF DIFFICULTY

a   b   c,d

Easy   Challenging

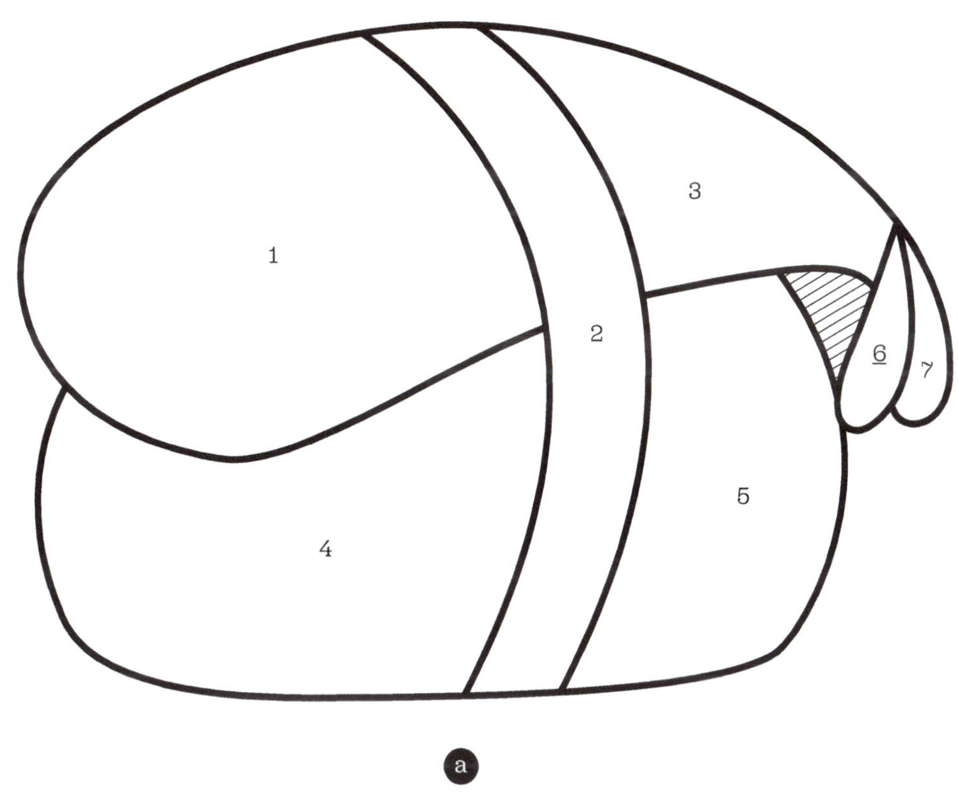

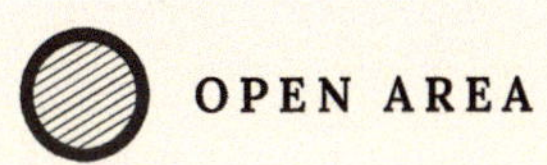
OPEN AREA

Nigiri

© 2022 Glass Class. All rights reserved. | glassclasspatterns.com

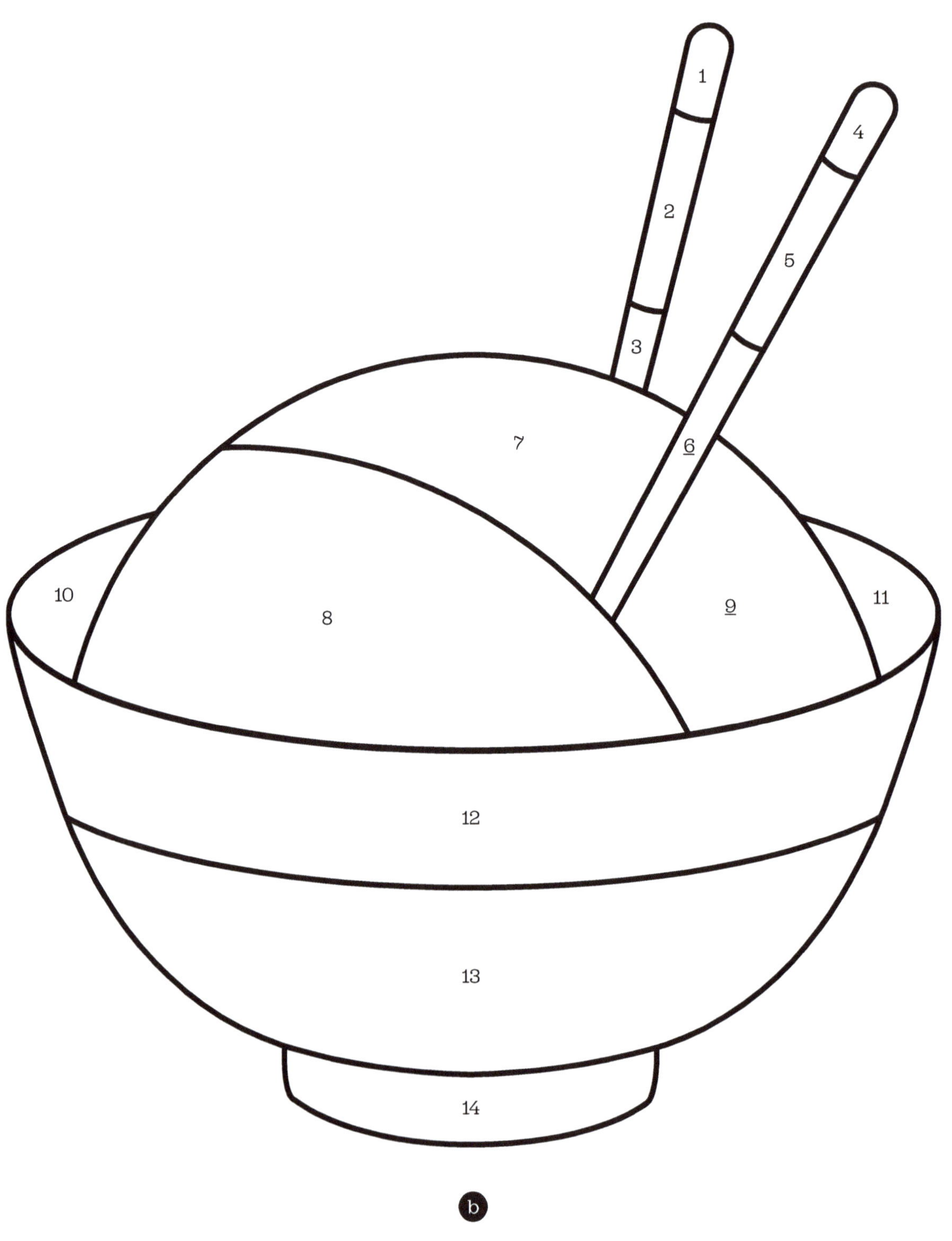

Bowl of rice

© 2022 Glass Class. All rights reserved. | glassclasspatterns.com

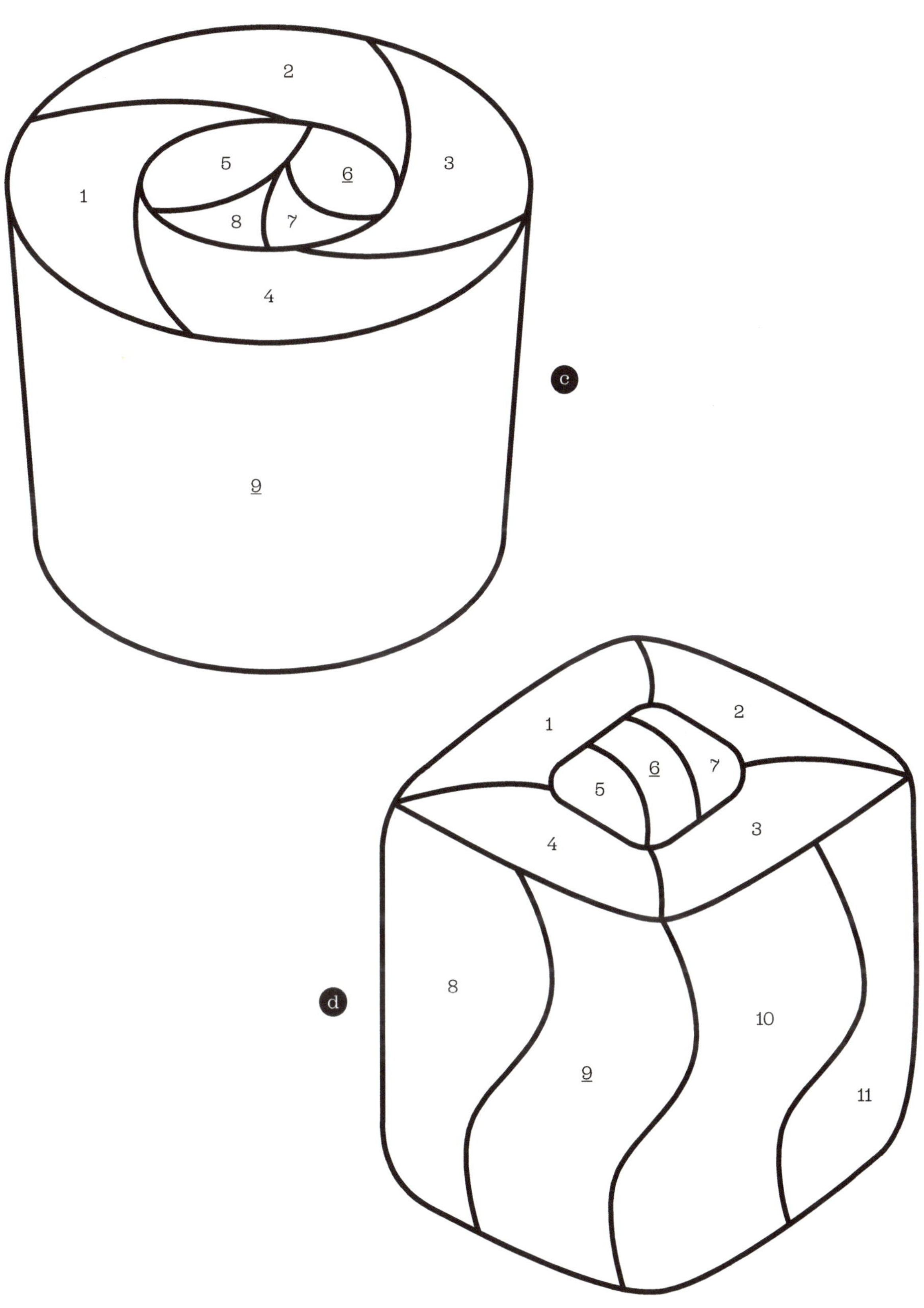

Sushi rolls

© 2022 Glass Class. All rights reserved. | glassclasspatterns.com

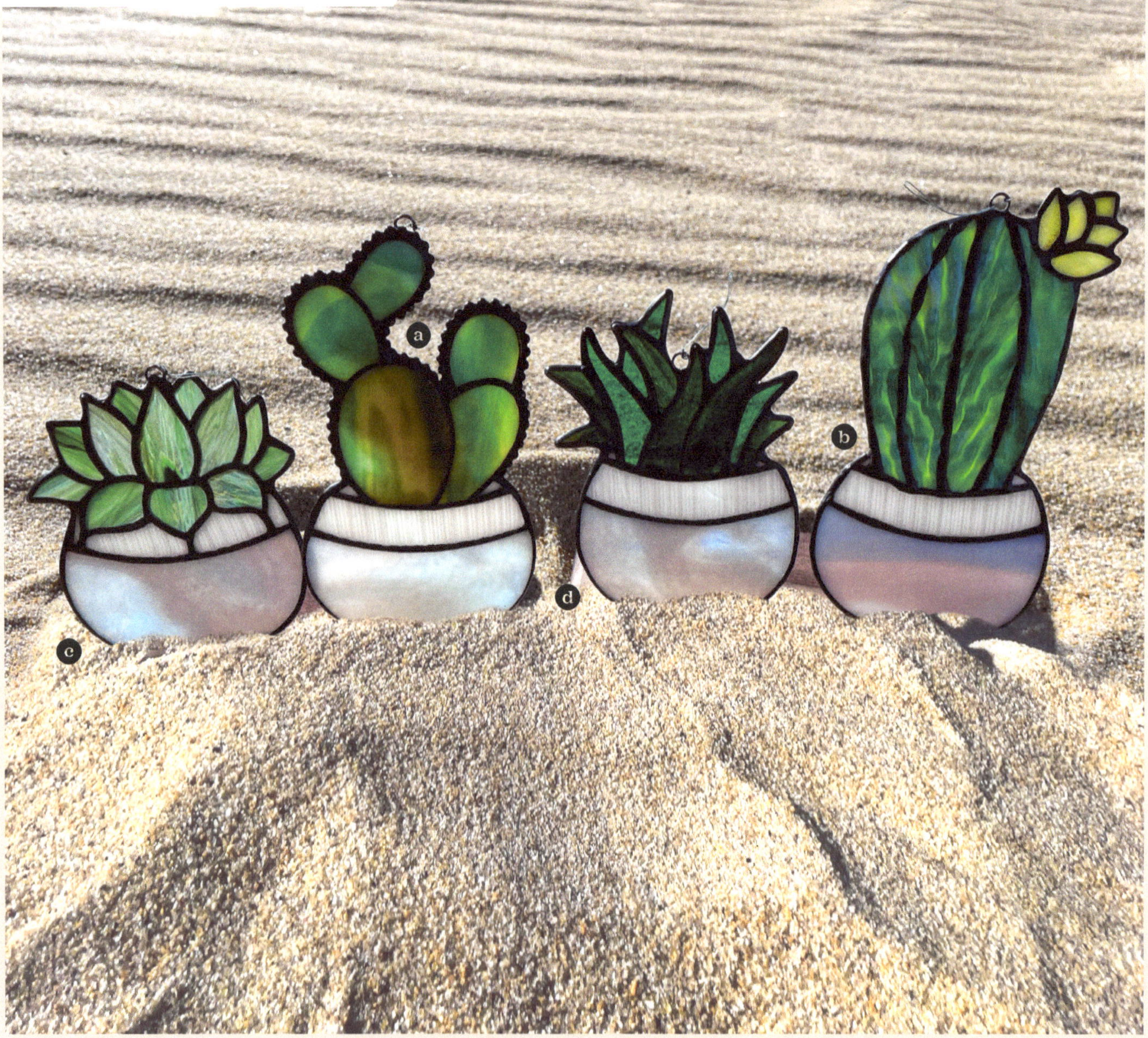

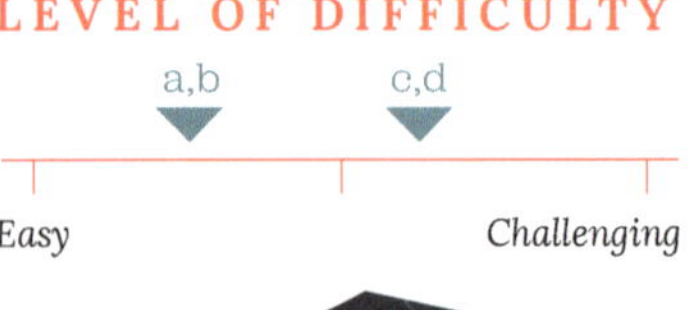

About these patterns

Succulents are known for their tenacity and strength. As standalone patterns or as a complete set, this garden represents growth, resilience, and uniqueness. You can display these pieces in an arrangement or hang them on a sunny window as the ultimate low-maintenance houseplants.

Heidi's tips

Use textured glass to add realism and individuality to each succulent variety.

To add detail like cactus spines, you can solder ball chain or short lengths of pre-tinned wire to the perimeter.

TOTAL NUMBER OF PIECES

a *9*   c *17*

b *13*   d *15*

FINISHED SIZE (approx.)

a *3.2" x 5.7"*   c *3.6" x 4"*

b *3.3" x 6.2"*   d *3.6" x 4.6"*

LEVEL OF DIFFICULTY

a,b   c,d

Easy   Challenging

Stained Glass Suncatchers

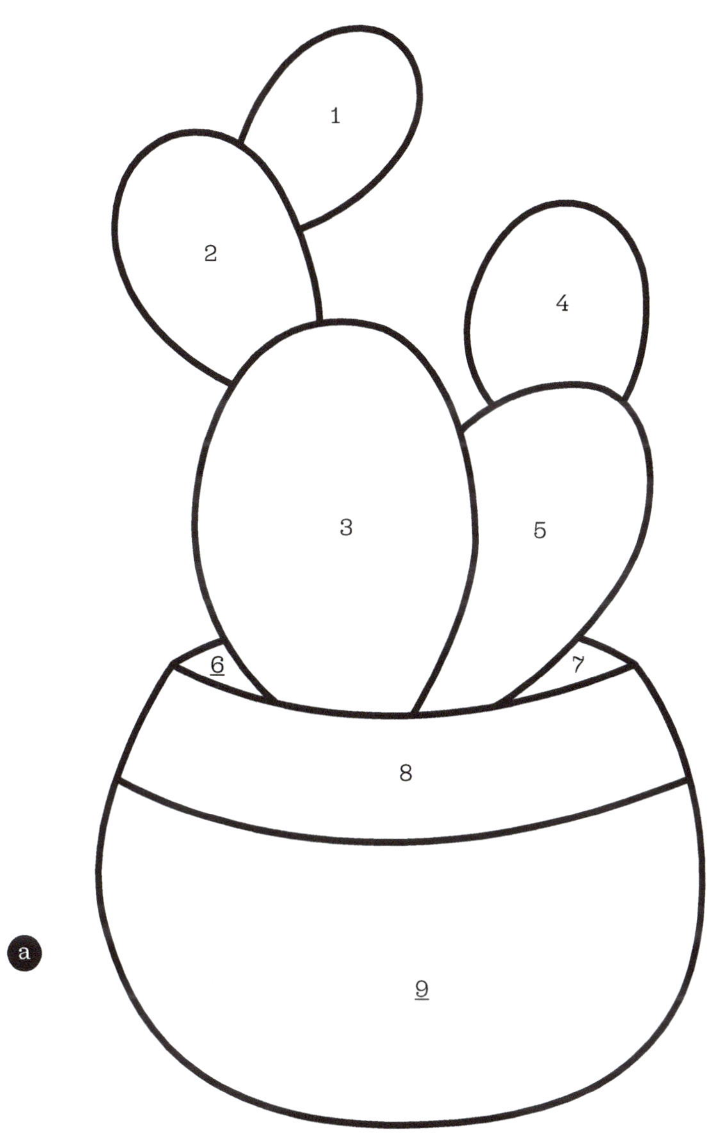

Prickly pear

© 2022 Glass Class. All rights reserved. | glassclasspatterns.com

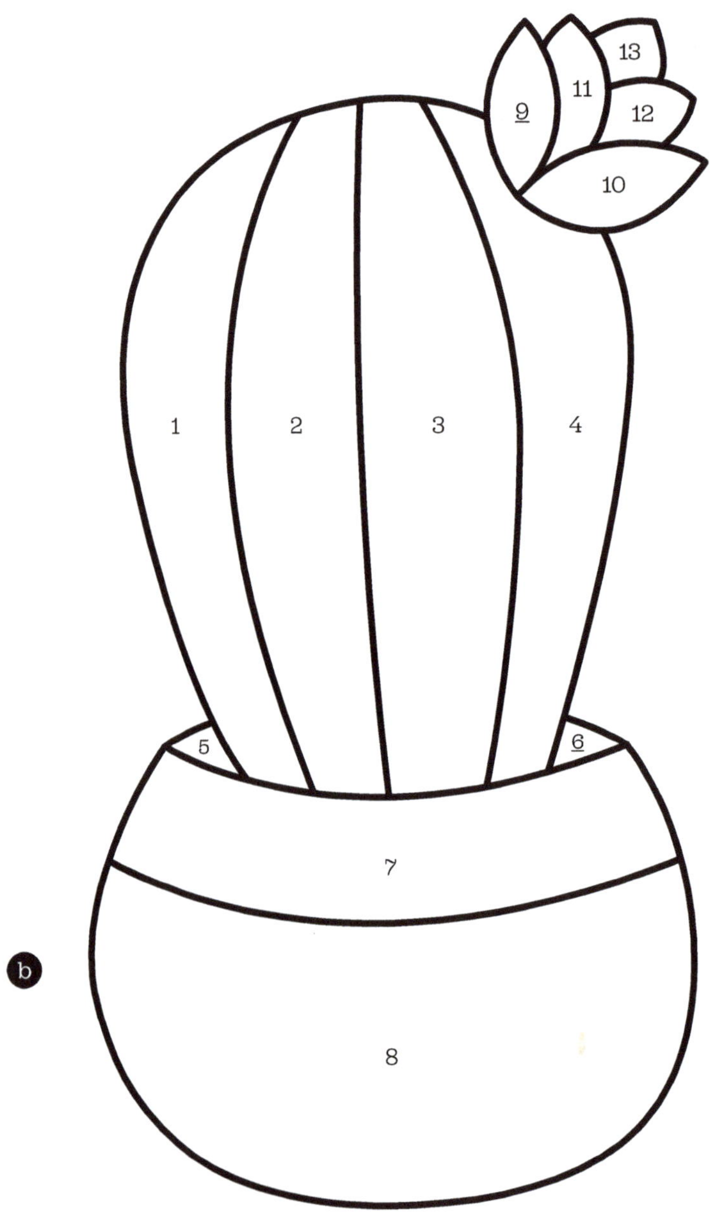

Cactus with flower

© 2022 Glass Class. All rights reserved. | glassclasspatterns.com

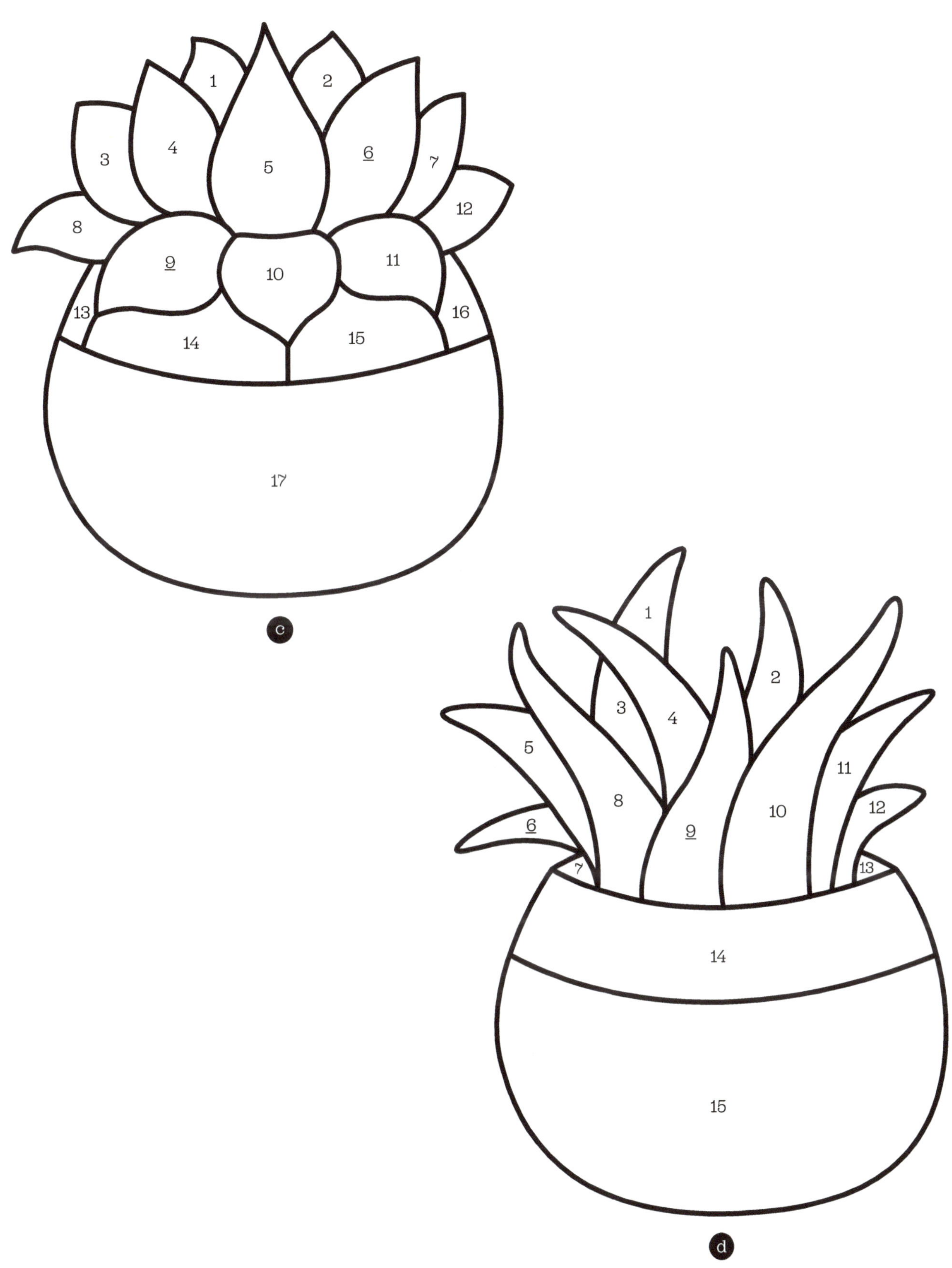

Succulents

© 2022 Glass Class. All rights reserved. | glassclasspatterns.com

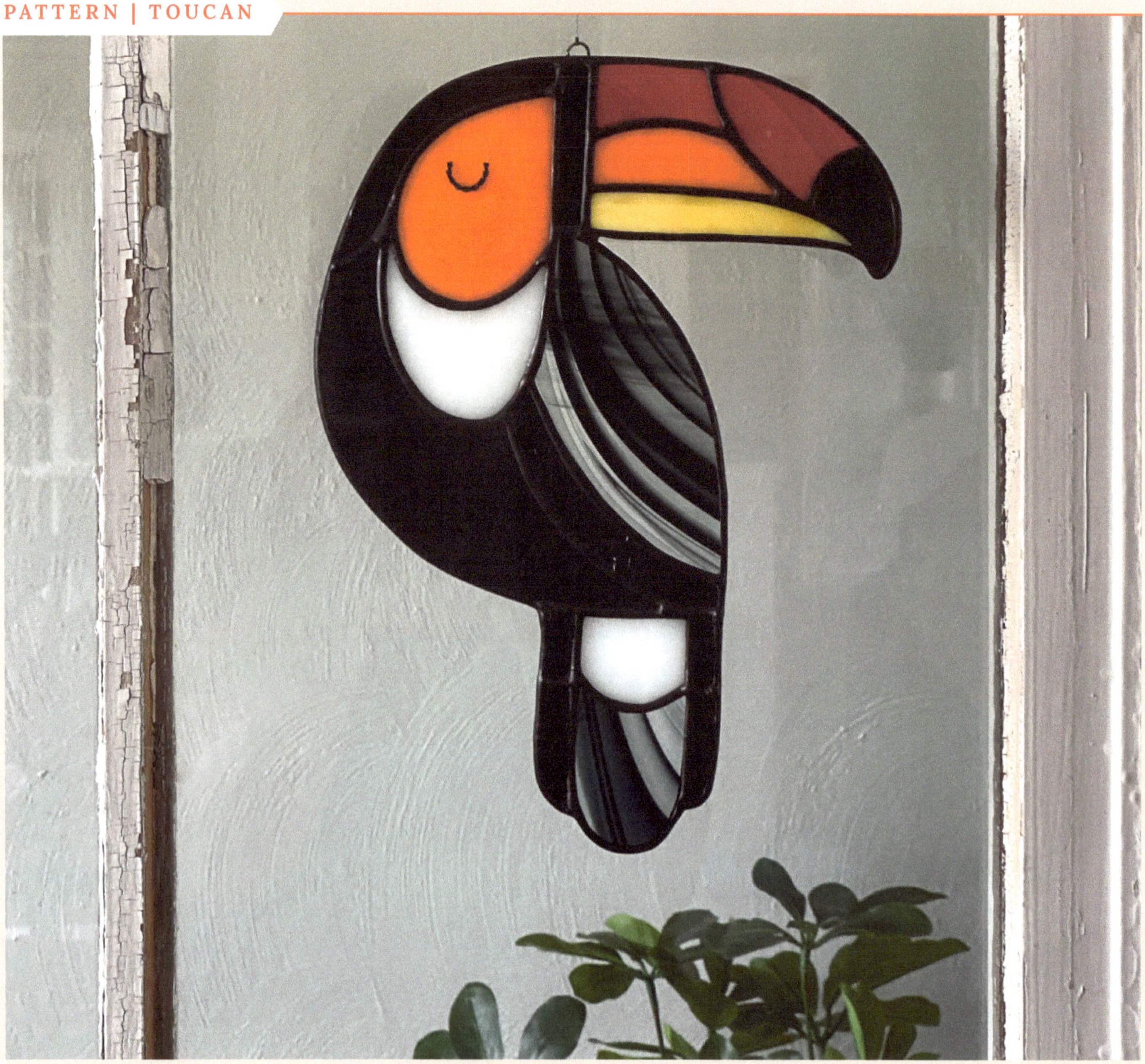

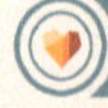

About this pattern

Known for its bright, colorful bill, the toucan represents communication and confidence. Let this suncatcher serve as a reminder that you deserve to be seen and heard, or gift it to someone special who's ready to step into the spotlight.

Heidi's tips

Use the texture and patterns in glass to suggest movement. Three different types of black glass were used for the body and wings of the sample to represent ruffled feathers.

Use wire to create an eye that reflects the mood of your bird. Follow this pattern, or draw your own shape on paper and bend the wire accordingly. You can twist two pieces of wire together to create a bolder eye. Adhere the wire to the glass using an industrial-strength adhesive meant for use with glass.

TOTAL NUMBER OF PIECES

18

FINISHED SIZE (approx.)

6.3" x 8.5"

LEVEL OF DIFFICULTY

Easy — Challenging

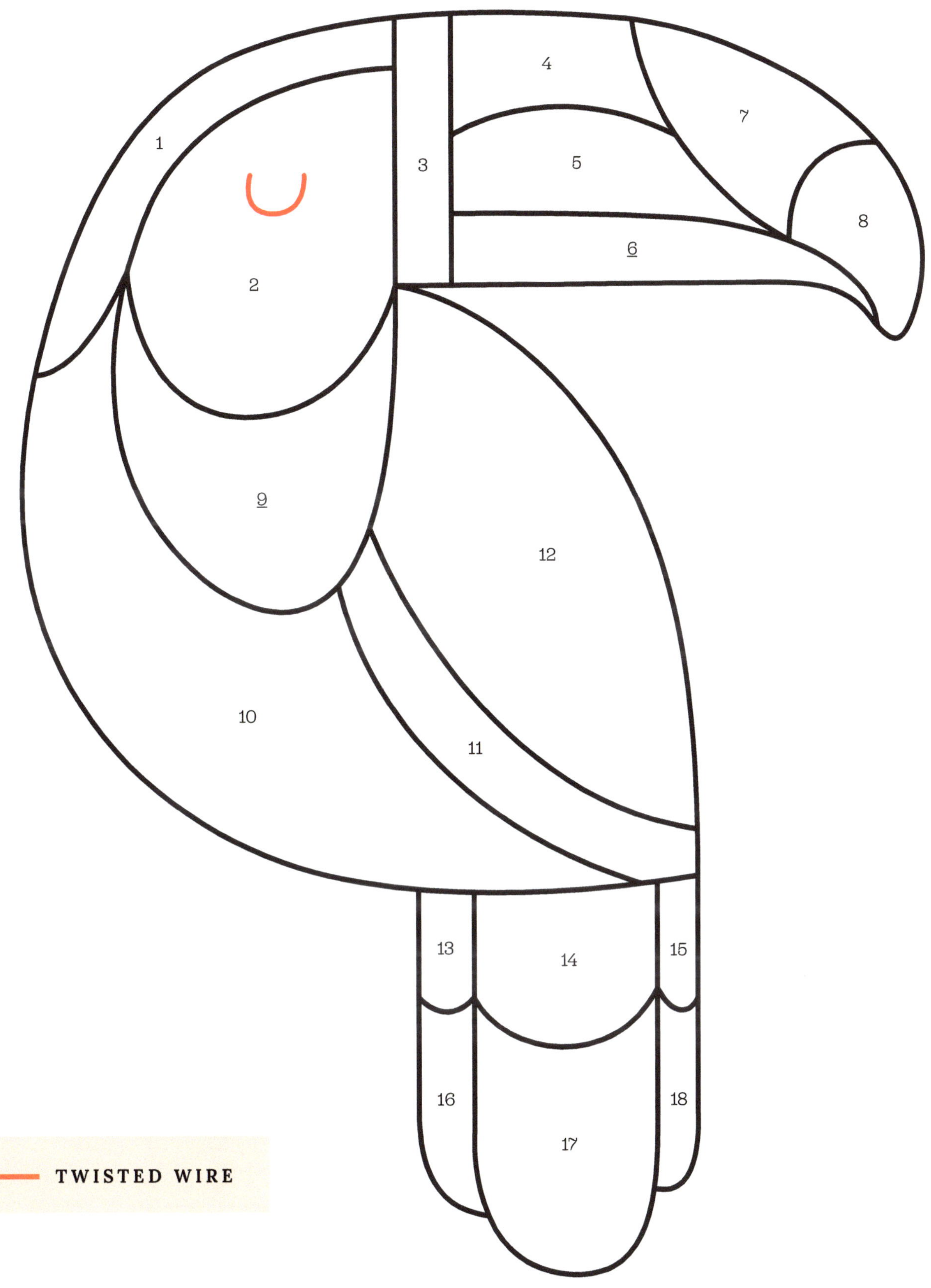

Toucan

© 2022 Glass Class. All rights reserved. | glassclasspatterns.com

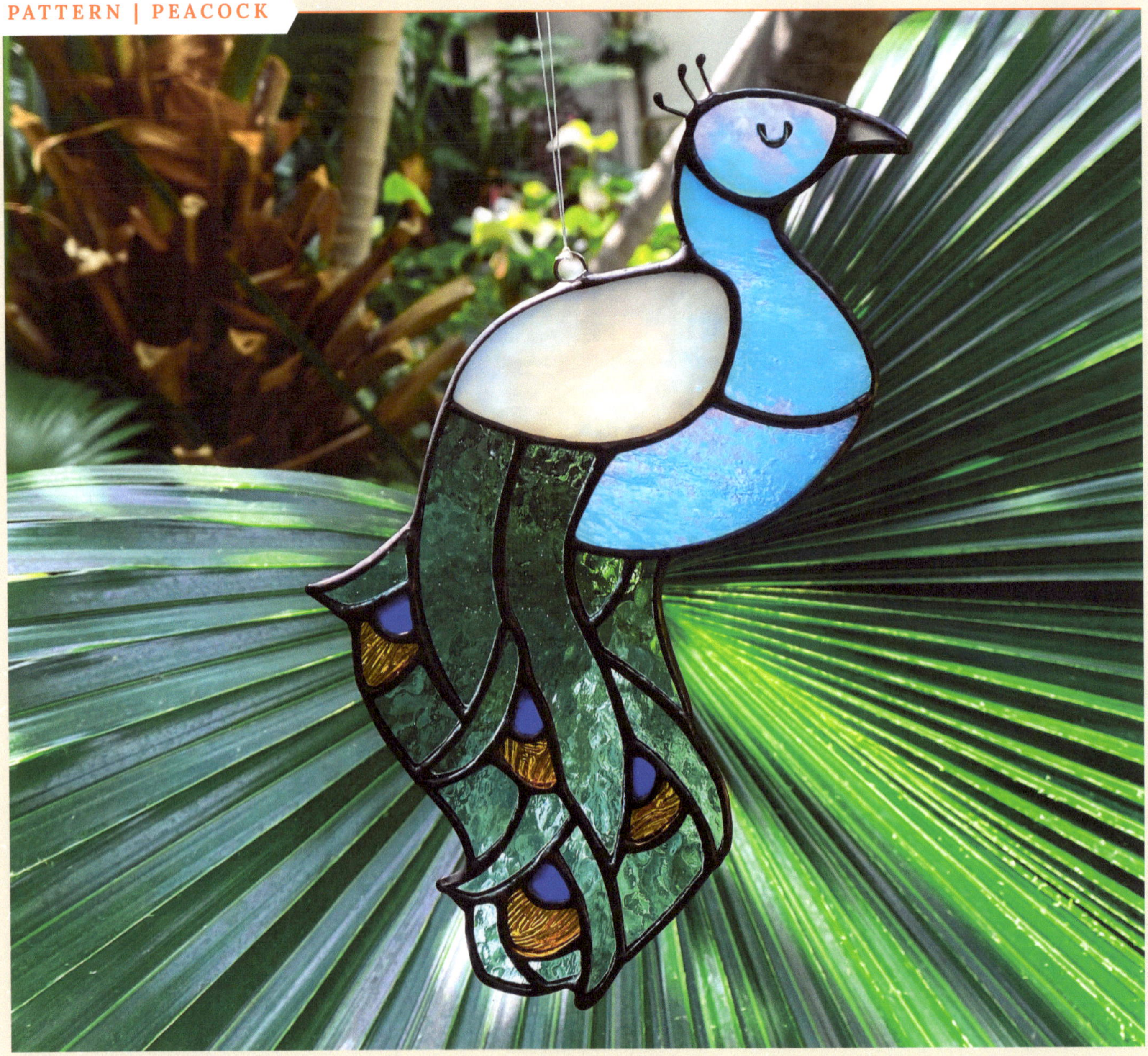

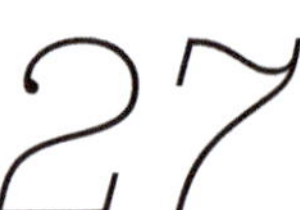

TOTAL NUMBER OF PIECES

27

FINISHED SIZE (approx.)

4.6" x 7.8"

LEVEL OF DIFFICULTY

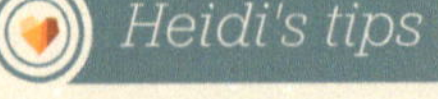

Easy   Challenging

About this pattern

Peacocks symbolize beauty, self-esteem, nobility, and good fortune. In this layout, the peacock's feathers are at rest; a fowl ready to wow the world. Use unique wiring to add flourishes and personality to your piece.

 *Heidi's tips*   Reference tips on page 54 to create eyes with twisted wire.

For the crest feathers at the top of the peacock's head, take three short lengths of wire and bend tiny loops at the end of each piece. Apply flux and fill the loops with drops of solder.

To achieve the small U-shape of the eye, bend your twisted wire around the tip of your needle-nose pliers.

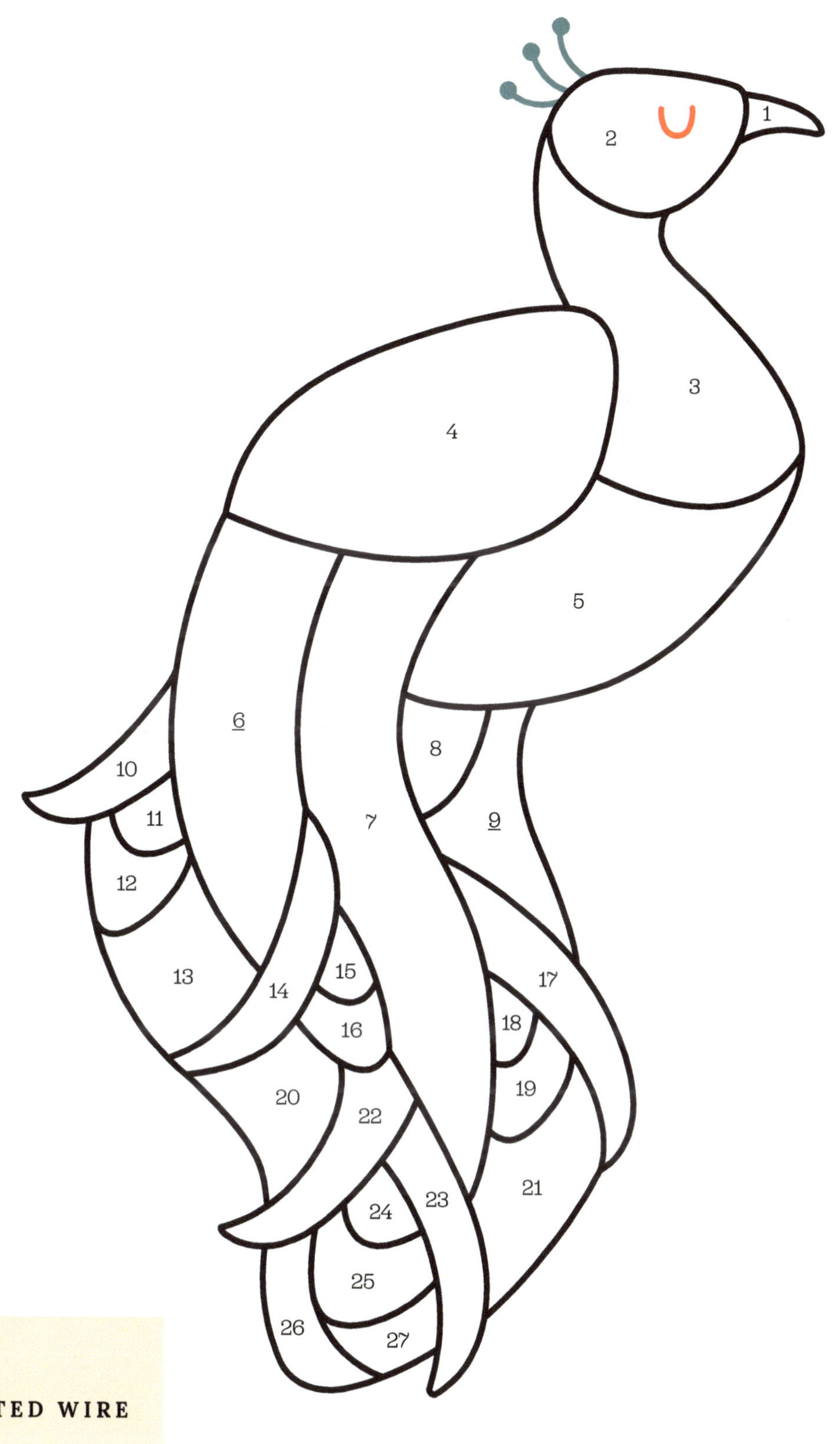

WIRE

TWISTED WIRE

Peacock

© 2022 Glass Class. All rights reserved. | glassclasspatterns.com

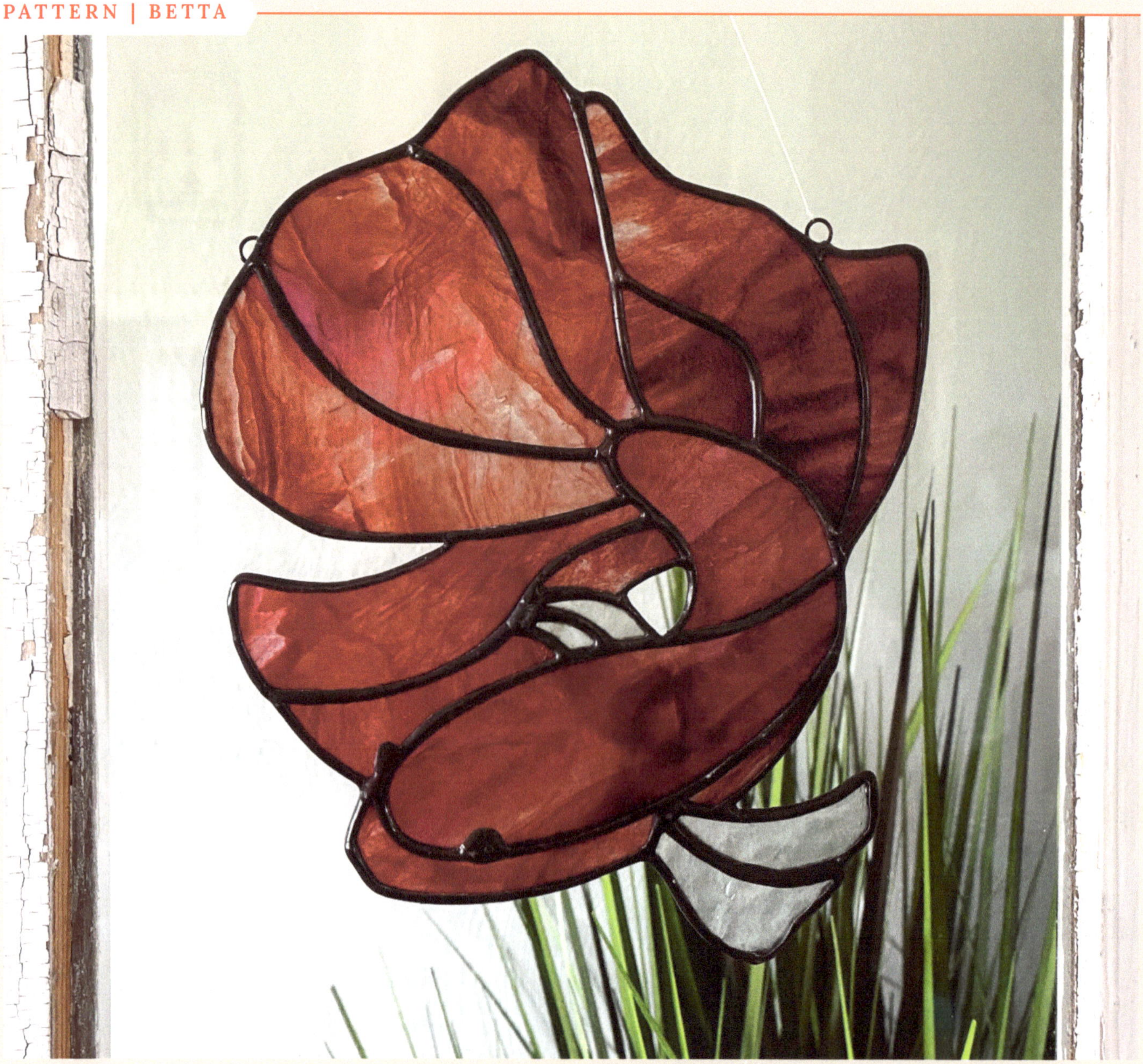

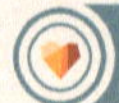

TOTAL NUMBER OF PIECES

17

FINISHED SIZE (approx.)

6.5" x 7.4"

LEVEL OF DIFFICULTY

Easy — Challenging

About this pattern

This pattern is an homage to Sarah's late, treasured betta fish, Pickle. Bettas symbolize individuality, strength, beauty, and defiance. They are known for their ability to thrive in harsh conditions. This suncatcher is ideal for the fierce and beautiful fighter in your life.

Heidi's tips

Because it is fairly large for a suncatcher, use two O-rings for hanging. This helps to evenly distribute the weight of the suncatcher.

Cut eyes for the betta from copper foil tape. With the adhesive side down, place the eyes where you would like them — preferably beside a solder bead — and smooth with your fid. Add a little flux and drop solder onto the eye. Then, melt the solder into the bead.

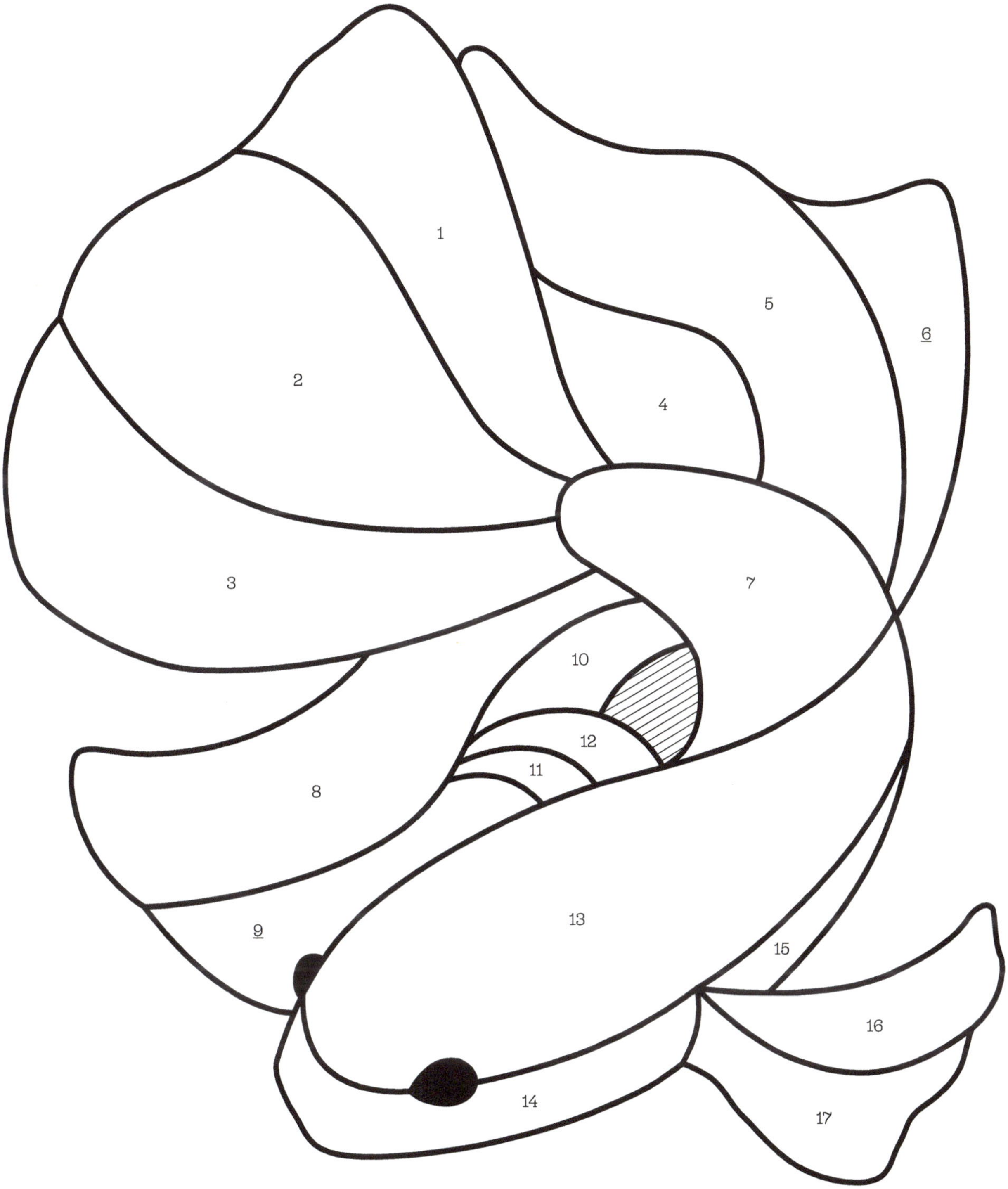

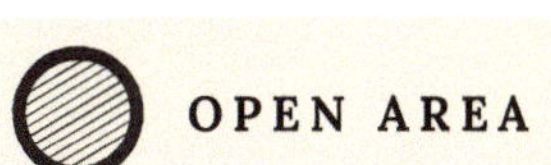

Betta

© 2022 Glass Class. All rights reserved. | glassclasspatterns.com

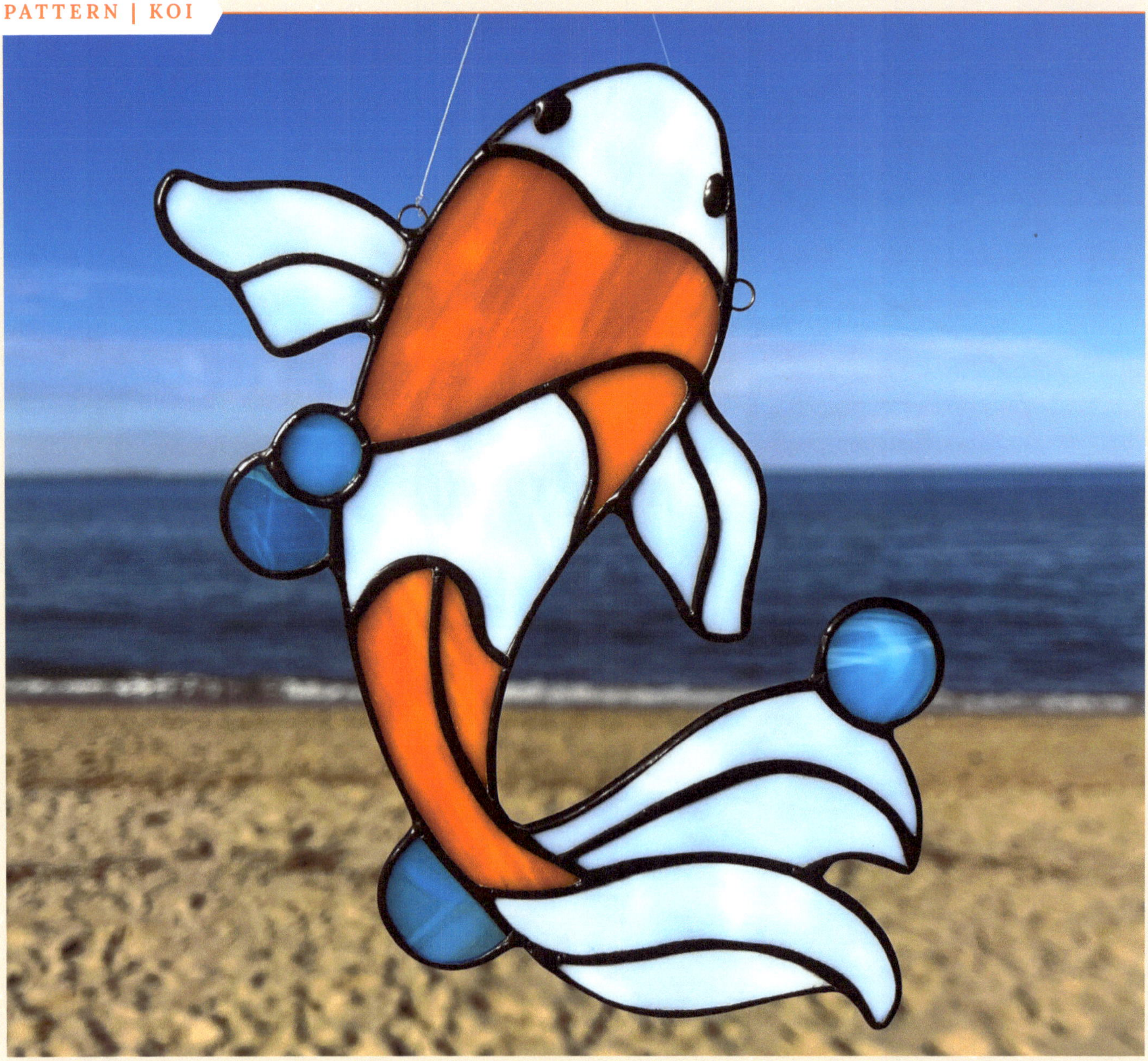

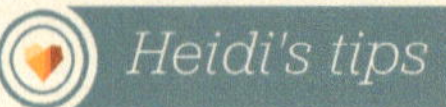

About this pattern

The koi fish symbolizes good fortune, success, and prosperity. The swimming koi, as designed in our suncatcher, also represents determination. It's easy to be inspired by the koi's beautiful coloring and meaning — good things come to those who keep swimming.

Heidi's tips

Reference tips on page 58 to create solder eyes.

There are deep inner cuts on a few of the pieces in this pattern. Don't be afraid to use your grinder to get a little deeper than you can comfortably cut — just make sure to adjust the piece next to it so that it fits tightly.

If you want this suncatcher to be realistic, do some research on the species you are depicting. This will help you replicate colors and patterns found in nature.

TOTAL NUMBER OF PIECES

18

FINISHED SIZE (approx.)

5.7" x 8.6"

LEVEL OF DIFFICULTY

Easy   Challenging

Stained Glass Suncatchers

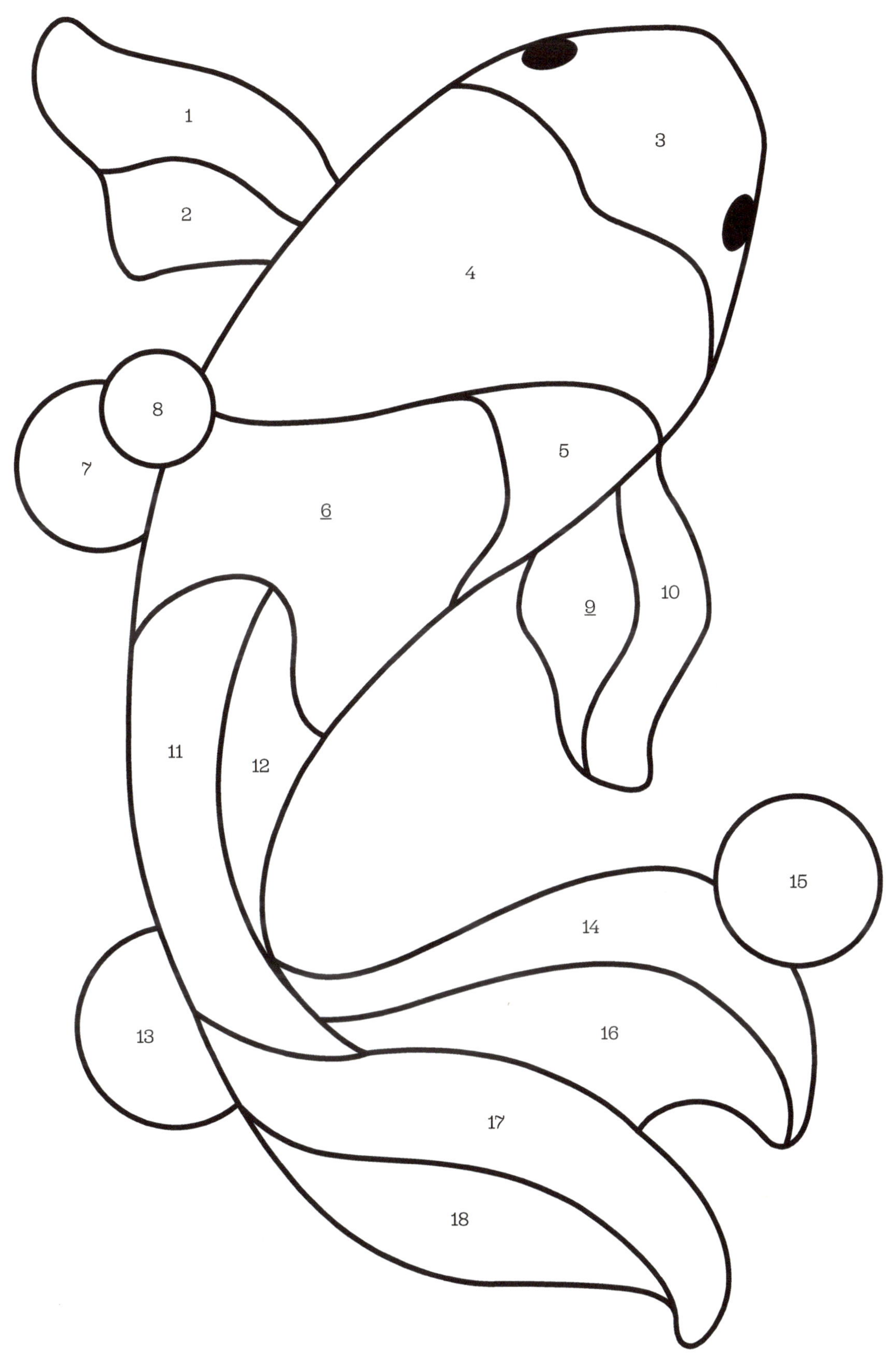

Koi

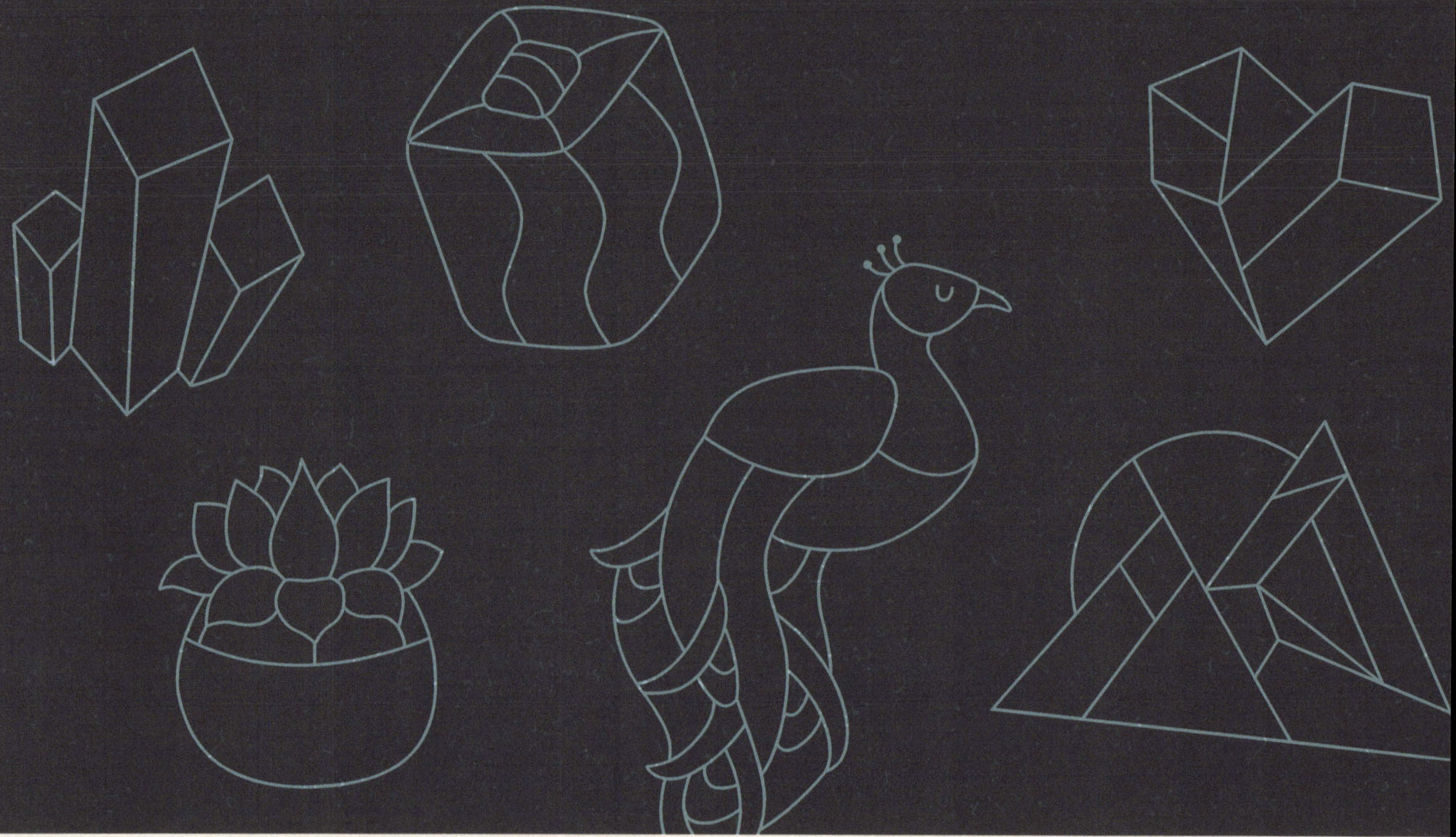

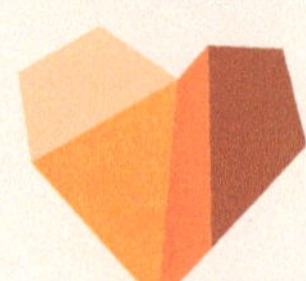

Made them all?

You rock! We'd love to see your work — post a photo
on social media and tag us **@glassclasspatterns**

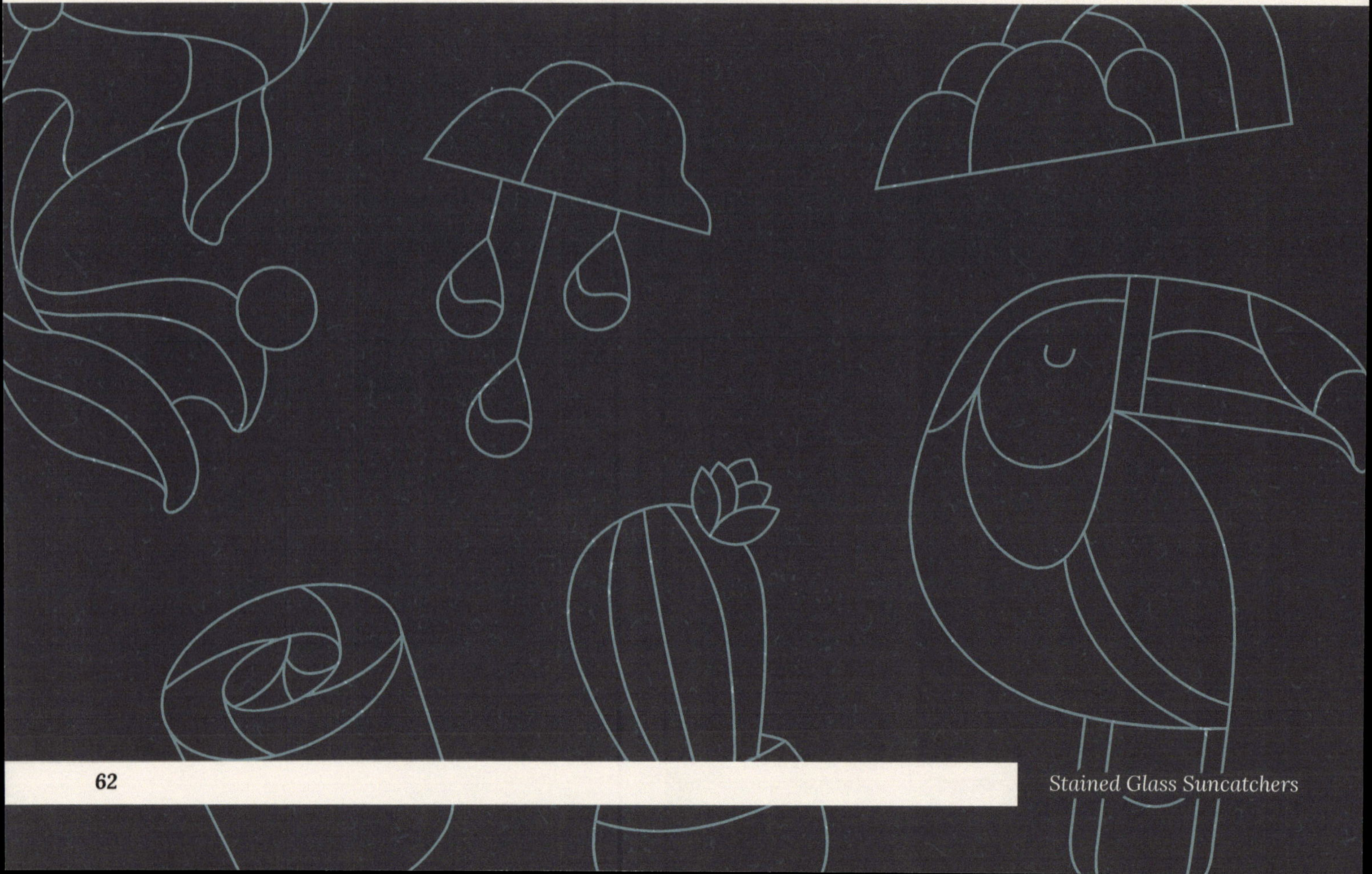

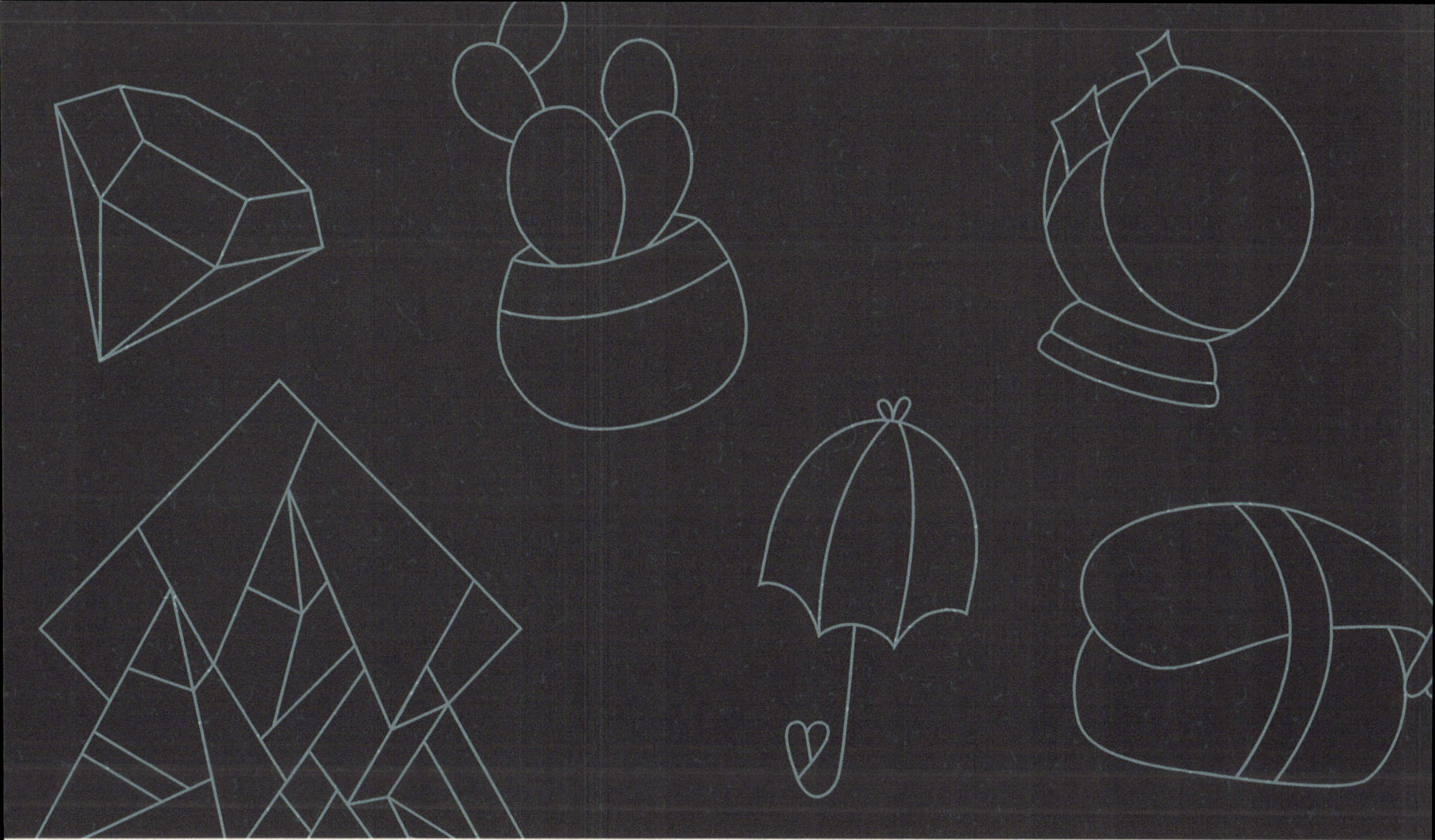

For new challenges and more patterns, visit our website:

GLASSCLASSPATTERNS.COM

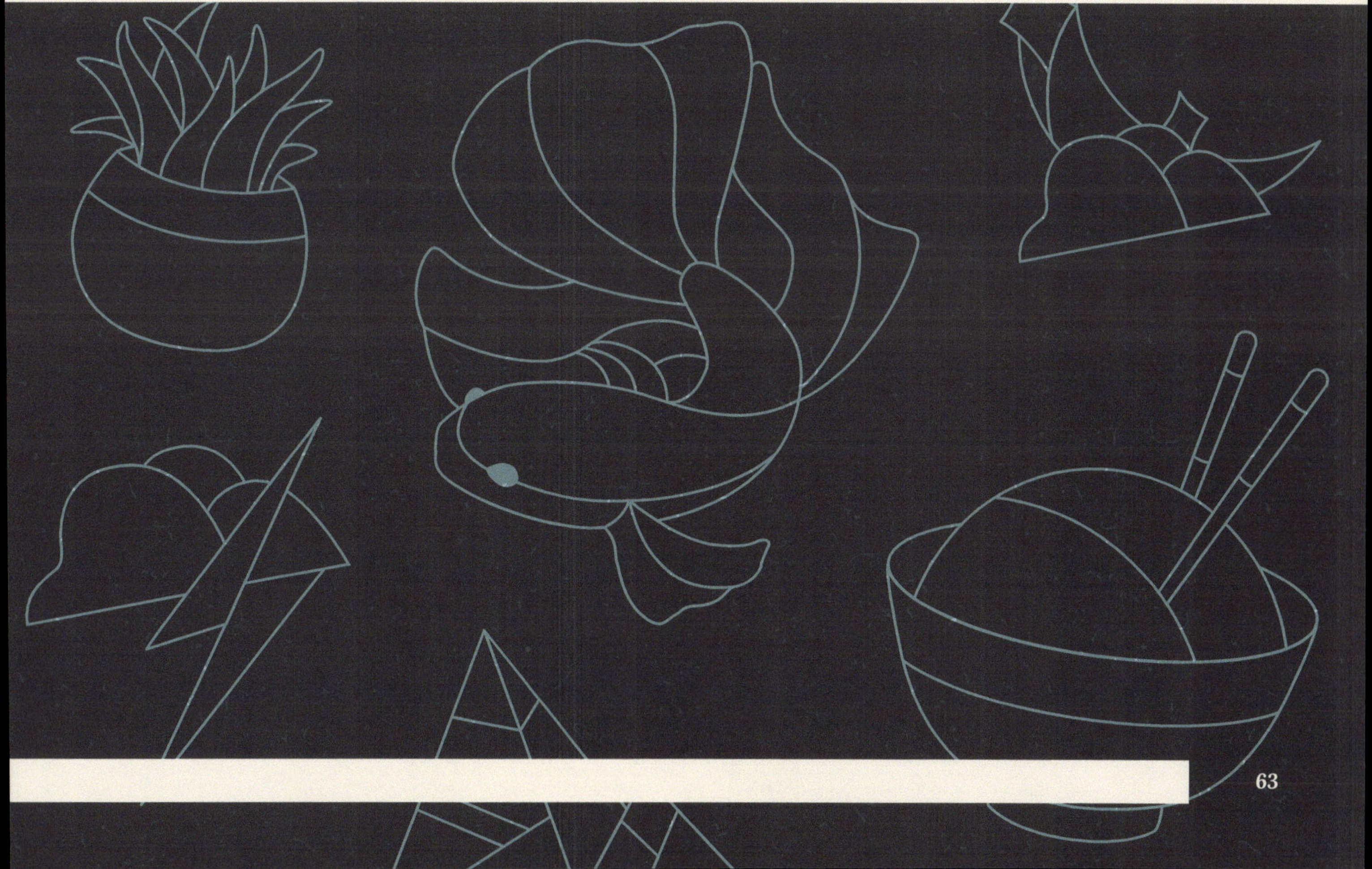

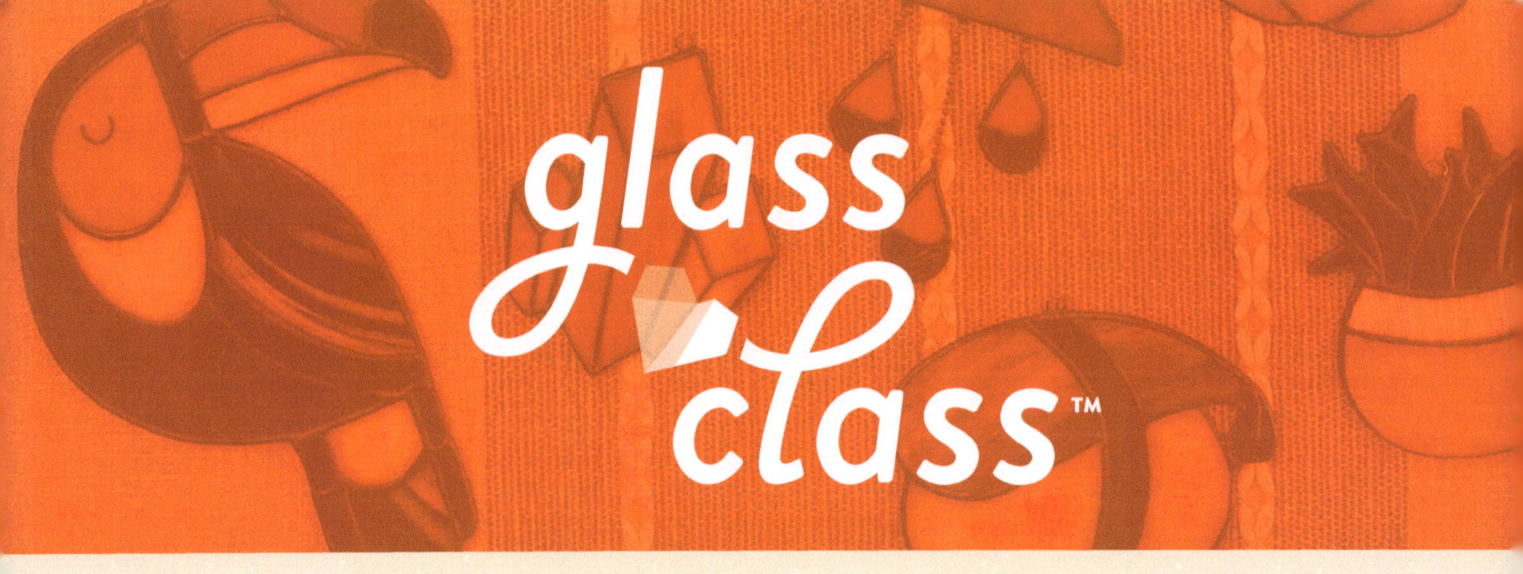

Copyright © 2022 Glass Class.   @glassclasspatterns   glassclasspatterns.com

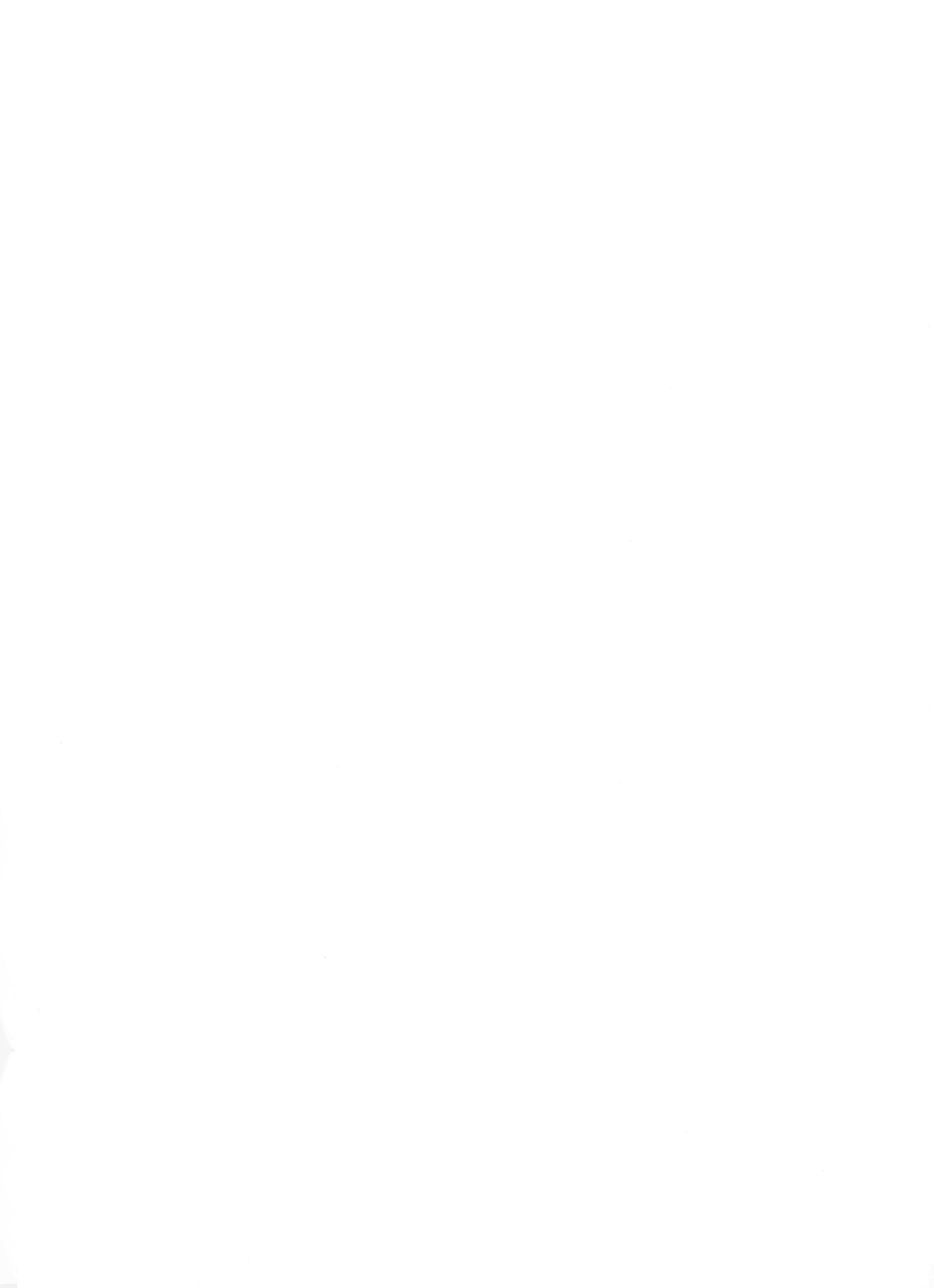

www.ingramcontent.com/pod-product-compliance
Lightning Source LLC
Chambersburg PA
CBHW042114030726

47599CB00002B/212